IMAGINED AGENCIES

By
Joseph Bulgatz

First published by Dog Ear Publishing
4011 Vincennes Road
Indianapolis, IN 46268
www.dogearpublishing.net

ISBN: 978-1-4575-6189-4

This book is printed on acid free paper.
Printed in the United States of America

INTRODUCTION

O ur lives are shaped by regulatory bodies to an extraordinary degree. Their number is so great that even a listing of their types is impressive: there are agencies, boards, bureaus, commissions, committees, councils, courts, directorates, groups, inspectors, institutes, leagues, offices, societies and systems. Each of these entities exercises some control over our activities, directly or indirectly; in one way or another they administer, adjudicate or simply attend. The quantity of rules and regulations they issue is vast, suggesting the endless shelves in Borges' "The Library." Consider, for example, the rules and regulations of the Internal Revenue Service, contained in no less than 50 volumes, aggregating many thousands of pages, and containing a mountain of information that deals only with the United States Income Tax. This is a world arcane to many, inhabited by men and women who claim expertise, speak their own language, foreign to many, sometimes called bureaucratese. In time, there may even appear an instructional program modeled on ESL—"Bureaucratese as a Second Language" it might be called. Courses will be given about agencies and their histories, treatises on various aspects will be written, and, as the subject grows in importance, some students may elect it as their major field of study. Eventually, it may even be possible to obtain a degree in the new field—"Agentology," it might be called.

In their number and influence agencies sometimes suggest a separate population of beings that exist in the lowest level of the atmosphere around our heads where they take turns directing our behavior. In this view, we are like large robots, clambering stiffly here and there while these true alter egos, like midget operators located behind our eyes stare ahead, turn the wheel, throw the switches and operate the brakes all in order to make our robotic bodies move, sit, stand, run, sleep, etc.

Attention must be paid to this subject because it is so influential in our lives and has received so little comment. As our ancestors lived close to the land, we now live close to innumerable, incorporeal governmental agencies that shape our behavior. While animal and plant species are declining in the biosphere (largely due to homo sapiens), these infosphere entities, composed, not of blood, tissue and bone, but of statutes, rules and regulations, proliferate. In the future, it is certain that they will grow in number and influence as legislation continues to be enacted and more and more human activity becomes subject to regulation. What that future may be is the subject of the following chapters. If the dry facts about present-day agencies may not secure that needed attention, some speculation about the future of these entities may prove to be more interesting.

Some of these imaginary agencies may be shaped by social forces ("The Obesity Police," "The Inspector General for TV"), others by financial considerations ("The Student Loan Agency, Tontine Fund"), still others have historical roots ("The Negotiable Fire Department").

Should these entities seem unrealistic, it is only necessary to travel back in time and imagine trying to explain to an audience in the 1890s what a department of motor vehicles is and how it operates. For those in that audience, travel consisted of shank's mare, riding on a horse, in a horse-drawn carriage, or—more rarely—on a train. To what extent could they imagine driving a car at 80 miles per hour on an interstate highway? Decades from now, as life grows more and more complicated, it is likely that there will be many agencies other than those now in existence and some of them may strike us as improbable.

Some researchers in psychology have already proposed a method for measuring the extent to which one's mental space is occupied by agency-related matters. Called "The Rubinson Coefficient," for one of its founders, it measures the amount of time that elapses before the subject's thoughts again turn to agencies. These intervals can vary considerably from one person to another. Some practicing lawyers record remarkably low coefficients while there is evidence that those who practice meditation are often able to increase theirs. As expected, the Speaker of the House of Representatives registered a very low coefficient, but many were surprised that President Trump's coefficient was rather high. Further investigation, however, revealed that this was an aberration and that whether his mind was focused on agencies or not, it was really preoccupied with Donald Trump.

Our increasing involvement with regulatory bodies represents a replacement of stimuli to some extent. Long ago, our ancestors looked to the gods or listened to them before they acted. Now, those gods have been replaced by other external forces in the form of governmental agencies. It is a hallmark of our times that where we once took direction from divinities that spoke to us from the heavens, we now obey administrative bodies in office buildings; where once we looked to the clouds for guidance, now we look across a desk to an impassive governmental clerk.

THE METAPHOR REVIEW BOARD

This fixture on the scene of governmental regulation did not come into existence without considerable dispute. Was it necessary, critics wondered, that a figure of speech be regulated? Wasn't this the special province of poets others asked? These questions showed how ignorant many were of the true nature and function of metaphor. The results of a limited polling corroborated the widespread ignorance. Most of those queried were surprised to learn of the central role of this figure of speech in cognition. Then, there were those (and they were more than a few) who expressed astonishment that they had been using metaphors throughout their lives, evoking that character in Moliere's "Le Bourgeois Gentilhomme" who exclaimed "Good Heavens, for more than forty years I have been speaking prose without knowing it." Coupled with these reactions was the fear that such a body would violate the freedom of speech provision in the Constitution. That objection soon disappeared, however, when it became clear that the agency would be advisory only, its purpose merely to uncover and correct metaphor abuse rather than to prohibit its use no matter how bad that abuse might be.

The debate turned in favor of the agency's proponents when they demonstrated how powerfully misleading a metaphor could be in Congressional budget debates. With surprising frequency these debates compared the enormously complicated federal budget to the simple household budget. Reasonable voices pointed out the problems with such a comparison. The federal government was not like an individual, among other things, because it was immortal, created and regulated money, maintained military forces and was engaged in many other activities unknown to individuals such as international negotiations and the setting of tariffs. The household budget was very simple, the federal budget enormously complicated.

Once established, the Board continued to showcase the budget metaphor to further demonstrate its method of operation. On its website, in advertisements in print media and on television and with sympathetic columnists they made a powerful case in the court of public opinion that misleading metaphors were a major problem needing attention. The metaphor was not simply a figure of speech, they argued, but was the means by which a mind extends the understanding to new subjects. The process was compared to mountain climbing: hand over hand we go; with every new hold we rise to a higher level from which we can see more than we did before. Each hold is a metaphor, the Board said, speaking both metaphorically and with irony. To extend one's knowledge to something new involves comparing it to something already known. The question is always "What is it like?" Even Einstein, in making his extraordinary discoveries, used the process when he imagined himself racing through space beside a light beam. Fantastic, one might say, but Einstein captured the possibility by recalling being in a speeding car, and then using that memory to imagine space travel; in short, by a metaphor.

In its analysis, The Board went on to show that a metaphor is always both true and false. While it extends one's understanding to the new thing by linking it with something already known, the two things are not identical and the extent of that difference may vary. In the beginning, the Board expressed this duality in numerical terms. So, for example, a metaphor was said to be 75% true and 25% false or misleading. In time, however, that calculus became less plausible, largely because it suggested a precision that did not fit the subject matter and was eventually replaced with a graphic—the phases of the moon. This proved a success, not only because the lunar cycle was familiar to everyone, but also because it had been in use for some time in consumer publications to evaluate everything from cars to pressure cookers and TV sets. Just as the moon was both bright and dark in each phase, so each metaphor, the Board argued, has both valid, useful information and information that is misleading. That the moon metaphor was no more precise than the percentages it replaced passed with little comment.

Every day the Board examined the stream of public utterances vigilantly looking for offending metaphors. It was a daunting task, but one that yielded astonishing results. Each misleading metaphor was presented in context, carefully analyzed, and the amount of misinformation estimated. Then they were ranked according to a scale running from 1 to 10, the numbers increasing with the amount of misinformation. A Misleading Metaphor of the Month was the occasion for some publicity, and even more was accorded to the Misleading Metaphor of the Year. These events caused considerable embarrassment to those who had used them publicly.

At the same time the Board sought to broaden its audience by inviting the public to propose metaphors for discussion. Those whose submissions were chosen enjoyed a small payment, a certificate honoring him or her and the usual feeling of pride that accompanies public recognition. In a few cases the name of the individual became attached to the metaphor submitted, assuring him or her of some lasting, if minor, fame.

Having established its basic jurisdiction, the Board took up a number of ancillary topics. It showed how a metaphor could become virtually useless through exaggeration or overuse. A favorite example was the use of the sinking of the Titanic steamship to characterize rather ordinary events in legislative discussions. So often was that catastrophe cited by legislators that it began to seem almost a standard part of every speech. Not far behind was the use of Armageddon, an event of enormous destruction with a Biblical provenance, to describe the possible consequences of such commonplace events as the licensing of pet cats or garbage collection re-scheduling. In a related fashion, the Board regularly drew attention to metaphors that continued to be used although that which was referred to had become obsolete. Examples of this were "poaching on another's preserve," "circling one's wagons," "siege warfare," and "a full quiver of arrows."

Although nominally a review agency responsible for studying the language as it presently existed, the Board's staff grew restless in time and struck out in new directions. In one such episode they decided that the Board should be the source of new metaphors as their need arose. In particular, they thought that new developments in technology called for new metaphors and so they decided it was their duty to invent some. They coined "toe fluttering" to signify posting on Facebook, for example, and tried to replace "surfing the internet" with "digital marathoning." But even though the Board went so far as to employ celebrities to use the new phrases, their efforts never met with real success, and the proposed new metaphors fell by the roadside.

Occasionally, the Board examined a particularly powerful metaphor. A striking example was the use by the French anthropologist Claude Levi-Strauss of flour and worms to evoke humanity's present course of self-destruction. When flour is stored in burlap bags and warehoused, he pointed out, a certain kind of worm soon appears in each bag. The worms rapidly grow in number until they reach a critical point at which they begin to secrete a poison that kills them all. We are those worms, Levi-Strauss suggested, and we long ago passed the point at which we began secreting the poisons that will cause our extinction. Much of the power of such a metaphor derives from the disparate nature of the two elements that are joined together. To assimilate humanity, arguably the most complex and dominant of beings, with helpless worms squirming in flour bags produces a particularly dramatic effect that might be described (metaphorically) as leveraging.

This and similar experiences led the Board to create a Metaphor Museum. Housed in a handsome classically styled building, the museum contained a number of interesting exhibits showing how some metaphors developed and operated sometimes with short films.

In a further exploration of the use of metaphor in public discourse the Board began to focus on prominent people and the manner in which they used this figure of speech. The discourse of elected officials, other statesmen and celebrities came under scrutiny. This may have been the beginning of some of the problems that eventually brought the Board into disrepute for the mixture of metaphor and personality could be explosive. By evaluating a public personality's use of metaphor, the Board was, in effect, criticizing him or her; for this there could be political consequences. Those campaigning for election or re-election, for example, might find themselves under fire for their poor use of metaphor, as evidenced by the Board's rating, while those who had a better rating could boast of it as an endorsement. This development was not lost on some of the political action committees that began to pressure the Board to endorse their candidates and criticize their opponents. Although this development tarnished the agency's reputation, it soon became clear that the Board's importance had been in decline for some time. One explanation was that the technological revolution had overtaken the agency and made its activities seem less urgent than they once were. Essentially a rating agency, it operated in a seat-of-the-pants manner rather than by exact calibration. In a world increasingly concerned with scientific and technological matters, such approximations seemed old-fashioned, less important, and, eventually, somewhat obsolete. Another explanation was that the use of metaphor in general had declined. As e-mail grew into the favored means of communication for many, brevity and conciseness replaced more elaborate and flowery locutions. To many it seemed as if Bach and Beethoven had been replaced by rap and jazz, Mozart by whistling.

THE REALITY ADJUSTMENT BOARD

The average person watches television 4.5 hours a day. If he sleeps 8 hours, that means he is looking at the screen about 28% of the time. That does not include screen time at the movies. The images seen during such long periods inevitably influence his behavior. Unconsciously, perhaps, he models his reactions to real situations on the way fictional characters react to similar stimuli on the screen. We are avatars of those imaginary beings that we have been watching so long and so intently. The process is subtle, incremental and long-lasting. In some ways, it is reminiscent of "The Invasion of The Body Snatchers," that classic film in which people were mysteriously taken over by alien forces, their appearance unaffected, but their identities radically changed.

This conditioning process affects everyone. It is passed on to children by parents who permit them to spend long hours before the TV. To an extraordinary degree, our sense of reality is modeled on that of fictional people, and so, therefore, is our behavior. Perhaps this trend is most pronounced with respect to mating behavior since screen fare deals overwhelmingly with love stories.

The first warnings about this transformation came from some psychologists and sociologists, but they drew little attention; it seemed a theoretical matter, and one that affected only a few people on the edges of society. That changed when the results of widespread testing became available showing how in almost every case our sense of reality had been altered. We were fundamentally different from our ancestors who lived in pre-electronic times, and the comparison showed that, in important ways, we had become their inferiors, less capable of handling problems, more inclined to behave like the fictional beings whose characteristics we had absorbed.

That was the problem that brought this Board into existence. Often referred to as a sister agency of The Information Control Commission, it is actually quite different. While both monitor the media, the former seeks to regulate volume while the latter, initially, only measured the extent to which a presentation diverged from reality. For that purpose the Board uses a concept called "The Reality Quotient," or "RQ." It is often said of that concept that it represents the meeting of the technical and the aesthetic. Upon review by the Board, each presentation was modified in two respects. First, a notice appeared at the beginning and at the end stating that it had been reviewed by the Board and setting forth the average degree to which the presentation departed from reality. Second, a subscript ran continuously at the bottom of the screen setting forth the RQ applicable to that scene, and colored so that an RQ from 1 to 3 was green, 4 to 7 yellow, and 8 to 10 red.

At first, a certain amount of confusion surrounded the Board. Those whose education included some philosophy concluded that the agency dealt with metaphysics, the study of ultimate reality, and, to the extent that reality is only a psychological construct, they were not completely wrong.

Using statistics and test results, the Board made a persuasive case that we had been captured by the media, our minds warped, and our common sense disabled. We had been subtly re-programmed with a new sense of reality, one that was artificial and false. Normal values had been upended; materialism was ascendant, consumption the order of the day, and one's life was evaluated, at death, solely in terms of the wealth that had been accumulated. Traditional religion was fading. The argument was made even more compelling when it compared the process to those virtual reality devices that had become so popular and, according to some critics, contributed to that very change.

There had been considerable opposition to the creation of this agency, much of it coming from the advertising industry and their clients. Since the placement of advertisements usually involved harmonizing the sales pitch with the underlying program, the frequent reminder that the program diverged from reality was at variance with the latter's claim to truth, if not an unraveling of the latter's claim to credibility.

Nevertheless, once it established a foothold in this contentious area, the Board succeeded in having its powers enlarged to include the testing of the degree to which a viewer's sense of reality had been dislocated and the administration of various training programs aimed at remedying the condition. There were some who were aware of their own sensory maladjustment and willingly took this training. Others were persuaded by friends, relatives, employers and others cognizant of the problem. Referrals by psychoanalysts accounted for many referrals, but there were also some from criminal court judges who were convinced that the defendants' behavior had its roots in television and the movies.

There remained a small sub-group of those whose sense of reality had been so profoundly altered that the usual training would have been ineffective. These were equipped with what looked like virtual headsets they were required to wear in accordance with a schedule. In effect, this arrangement re-programmed the wearer's sensory input so that his sense of reality was eventually adjusted. Unfortunately, these headsets quickly became seen as a badge of mental deficiency and those who wore them were hooted at, and became the targets of derisory comments. The testing methods were unique, consisting of essays followed by multiple choice answers. Each essay was modeled on the basic situation in a well-known TV program or film, and the answers included one that closely followed the responses of the characters in that story. To a remarkable degree, those taking the tests chose the same answer as the fictional character did, proof that their natural sense of reality had been perverted. The same tests were used to determine when the subject had been rehabilitated. Unfortunately, crib sheets and test guides soon appeared making it easy to cheat on these tests. The Board tried to control the situation by changing the tests from time to time.

Rehabilitation was rigorous, requiring the subject to abstain from any TV viewing for a minimum of one month. There were many stories of the difficulties experienced by those who took these programs, hysteria, sobbing, uncontrollable trembling and severe insomnia. Comparisons were made with those who struggled with drug addiction and alcoholism. Not all were equal to the challenge and dropped out. Such circumstances led to the development of a number of facilities around the country where those who suffered from what was now called "Screen Syndrome," could receive intensive treatment for their affliction. Operated like basic military training camps, they devoted all their activities towards one goal—the permanent weaning away from all television and cinematic influences. Included in these organized distractions were wood-working, knitting and musical instruction.

To insure that those who took this training remained television-free, they were required to wear a device that looked like a wrist-watch or the new fit-bit, and recorded times spent before a TV set or a movie screen. These recordings were reviewed monthly, and, if they showed a certain amount of viewing, the wearer was required to go for additional training.

In aid of some of these measures, the Board obtained court orders allowing its representatives to enter one's home and remove all television sets found there. Some of the representatives engaged in this activity went further and trashed the sets at the front door for added effect.

Other activities were of almost a political nature, but also sought to intervene in the process by which viewers' sense of identity was being distorted. These included demonstrations at the premieres of some films where placards were waved and sit-downs occurred. On several occasions Board employees appeared in front of the theaters costumed and made up to look like the film's main characters and carried on in ways diametrically opposed to those in the film.

When the film was a typical western, for example, the demonstrators appeared in drag.

THE UNION OF CHARITABLE
ORGANIZATIONS

Consolidation had been under way in the private corporate sector for some time, and it was only natural that the same forces would have their way in this field. Not only did consolidation make for greater efficiency and a consequent reduction in costs, the new body could speak more forcefully and apply much more pressure than any of its constituent members could acting alone. And then, there were the tax implications. That there was a close relationship between charitable contributions and the income tax had always been understood. It was usually in December, as the tax year was drawing to a close, that the money started coming in to the various charities, prompted by the need taxpayers felt to claim deductions from gross income, as the window of time was closing. What those contributions might have amounted to in the absence of their deductibility was a subject no one cared to consider, although they would certainly have been much less.

It was the genius of those in the Union to see the possibility that tax treatment was not carved in stone, but might be increased. From the beginning, therefore, the Union sought, by lobbying, amendments to the Internal Revenue Code that would make charitable contributions more valuable. Having gathered together all the resources of the many various charities, it proved to be a persuasive force in the halls of Congress.

The proposals varied. At one extreme the Union argued for a radical change in the way charitable contributions were deducted, not from gross income, but from the actual tax due, dollar for dollar. Although such a bill was regularly introduced, it was generally understood that it had no real chance of passage and represented merely an act of courtesy to the Union. Refusing to give up, however, the Union modified the bill so that the value of the deduction from the tax due was scaled down from dollar-to-dollar at first by half and then further. None of these changes, however, succeeded in getting the bill enacted.

Under more serious consideration was a proposal that the amount of charitable deductions be subject to annual adjustment in response to changes in the Consumer Price Index taking place between the time of the contribution and the end of the year. Under such a plan the extent to which charitable contributions were eroded as a result of inflation in that year would be restored, thereby augmenting their value.

Another proposal was modeled on the income averaging scheme found in the Code some years ago. As applied in this context, a taxpayer with an extraordinary amount of charitable contribution in a given tax year would have the option of carrying some of it forward into later years and use it then. This proposal was also given serious consideration.

In an even more imaginative proposal, the Union sought to increase the value of the deduction to an individual on a sui generis basis. In principle, if the individual could demonstrate how the charity benefited him, he might increase the value of that deduction. So, for example, someone suffering from cancer who contributed to a cancer research organization that qualified, would be eligible for a greater credit. The formula for calculating that increase was complex depending on such factors as age, the severity of the condition, life expectancy, and other matters.

Lobbying was not limited to the income tax. As important were the Union's efforts to change the gift tax. Under existing law, a gift up to $13,000 a year was free of tax. The Union lobbied strenuously to increase that limit, proposing various bills that removed the dollar limit, increased it to a greater amount, or, as with its income tax proposals, a functional change geared to changes in the Consumer Price Index. Nor were the Union's efforts confined to the gift tax limit. Other proposals aimed at nothing less than easing the strict definition of a gift, so that it would include a transaction in which the donor received some consideration. Similar efforts sought changes with respect to the estate tax that would, variously, raise the value of the estate before that tax kicked in, increase deductions and lower the rate.

The considerable presence and substantial treasury of the Union were felt elsewhere than in the legislative arena. The organization's advertising campaign was impressive, used the most glittering celebrities as spokesmen and women and reached out everywhere. On television it produced unforgettable segments that appeared on such special occasions as the Super Bowl, Christmas eve and Presidential addresses to the nation. The overall effect of such advertising was to persuade the public that charitable giving was an important part of life. Coordinated with that program was an ongoing telephone campaign in which almost everyone found himself or herself subject to eloquent pleas for further contributions. In addition, agents sought to persuade those in higher income levels to sign up for monthly payments through their credit cards or by an automatic deduction from their salaries. These efforts met with some success.

Influential as it was, however, the Union was not always able to maintain harmony among its constituent organizations. Part of the conflict could be traced to the way the Union's annual income was apportioned. Inevitably, there were members who felt that they were not receiving their proper share and that others were receiving more than theirs. This may have been due to memories of the time before the Union came on the scene when each charity was vying with the others for contributions, but it was also due to the fact that certain charities, almost by definition, were at loggerheads with others. As an example of this strife, an organization dedicated to the rehabilitation of drug addicts could not be comfortably harnessed with another aiming at encouraging the use of marijuana, even in such a large and varied body as the Union.

Still, there were those who regretted the change and thought back affectionately to the colorful variety of charities in the old days. Then, each entity had its own character, separate and apart from the others. Now there was only the monolith of the Union. It was as if a lush field containing all sorts of trees and plants had been cleared and paved over; in its place there had been erected a huge, faceless concrete tower.

THE GENTRIFICATION BUREAU

"**G**en-tri-fi-cation—Restoration of deteriorated urban property, esp. in working-class neighborhoods by the middle and upper classes."

This extraordinary agency seeks to emulate, orchestrate and apply those natural processes that had long been in operation, but were poorly understood and never under control. Urban neighborhoods seemed subject to a special kind of dynamic in which some became "hot," and others faded. Williamsburg and Bushwick were good examples, but, going further back further in time, the East Village was an even better example. The creation of this bureau was intended both to acknowledge the forces at work in this process and apply them systematically to designated areas.

To a certain extent, the new agency was a descendant of the old Slum Clearance Committee. An entity with an unhappy reputation, that Committee used the bulldozer to accomplish what might also be called gentrification. Those displaced by demolition were usually from the lower classes, and those moving in to the new, replacement houses from the middle or upper classes. This history gave ammunition to the critics of the new agency who battled hard to prevent what they claimed was a campaign against the poor. More points were scored when the critics drew attention to the implications of the Bureau's name: the "gentry" contemplated by the process were, strictly speaking, the nobility, the carriage trade, implications at variance with the Bureau's goals. In time, however, after some placard-waving, a sit-in, and a parade, that opposition faded away. There remained some uncertainty, however, as to the relationship between the Bureau and such regulatory bodies as the City Planning Commission. When it became clear that the Bureau's jurisdiction made it subordinate to those bodies the last remnants of opposition disappeared and the agency was ready to proceed.

Its first goal was to understand the process; why had certain areas become gentrified? What were the forces at work? Once they were identified and understood, the Bureau set about applying them, as far as practicable, to new areas. The selection of those new areas did not want for candidates. As news of the plan spread, a large number of proposals came in from a variety of city fathers, each one with an interest in upgrading the district he or she represented. All the members of the City Council were heard from, as well as Assemblymen and Senators, each clamoring for his or her district. But these officials were only part of the onslaught, for businessmen, professionals, store owners and others saw how they would profit from the transformation.

In choosing the areas to work on, the Bureau applied certain standards with respect to transportation and architecture. Any evidence that gentrification was occurring naturally, was cause for rejection since the staff insisted that they bear sole responsibility for the change. Concerning transportation, there was, initially, a division of opinion among the staff members as to whether or not the area should be well-served by subway and bus lines. Those opposed pointed to the situation of the Bronx where Riverdale, in the remote northwest, with little public transportation, is an upscale neighborhood, and Mott Haven, in the southern part of the borough, although close to mid-Manhattan and rich in transportation connections, has a very poor reputation. Eventually, an accommodation was made between the two groups.

Once chosen, the Bureau began the real work of gentrification. The process was essentially cosmetic since the agency could not simply move out the poor and under classes and replace them with the middle and upper classes. That, in effect, had been the policy of the Slum Clearance Committee, a policy long in disfavor. The Bureau could, however, create the appearance of middle class life by bringing in certain uses emblematic of that life. In this way, the agency arranged for at least one Starbuck's coffee shop on a major street, several upscale ethnic restaurants that were favorably reviewed, a few art galleries and health clubs, and at least one night spot with live music at which a number of celebrities regularly hung out (thanks to the hard work of the Bureau's publicity agent). A campaign was begun to induce Whole Foods to open a branch in the area. Steps were also taken to make some of the largest apartment buildings, which had become rather dilapidated, appear more elegant. Uniformed doormen appeared, handsome awnings fitted with brass hardware were stretched across the sidewalk, tired old doors gave way to splendid entrances with stained glass and names evocative of swanky districts in Paris and London were etched into corner stones.

Gentrification also involved the removal of uses that were inconsistent with the makeover. Towards this end certain stores were either helped to relocate or else bought out and closed. Among these were 99 cent stores, those dealing in used merchandise, pizza parlors and some bars devoted to hard drinking. Steps were taken to affix a new name to the area. For this purpose, a contest was begun with a substantial prize to the person who came up with the best name. The contest itself generated a certain amount of publicity, and thereafter the Bureau's publicity agent worked tirelessly to keep the new name in print and in the other media.

In addition, well-known people were encouraged to move into the area by offering to pay some or all of the new rent pursuant to a formula in which the amount paid would be in direct proportion to his or her celebrity. Financial assistance was also available for any well-known figure interested in buying a coop, condo, or an actual house. This activity was later enlarged to include those who the Bureau had identified as being among the pioneers and influential people in the transformation of areas previously gentrified.

Some or all of these commercial undertakings could not have taken place without generous subsidies from the Bureau which pursued its goal with a lavish hand. It may well be asked where was all this largesse coming from? The Bureau's treasury was substantial, for behind the agency stood a number of wealthy individuals and firms committed to see the area rise in value and certain to profit from it. To them it looked less like a gamble and more like a solid investment. As the neighborhood changed and the poor left, rental income from the new middle class tenants in the same apartments would rise. Sites could be acquired at reasonable costs and improved with new, high rise residential towers in which market rents, formerly a novelty here, could be charged, or, if the units were coops or condos, sold at market prices.

While planned gentrification was widely admired and seemed to have a bright future, it turned out to be vulnerable in unforeseen ways. Whatever social, economic and racial diversity may have existed in the area before the process began tended to disappear. It was as if some huge cultural steam-roller had flattened everything, leaving behind a much less interesting landscape. As the gentrifiers moved in, the poor, the blacks and the ethnics moved out. In the end, it turned out to be nothing more than a sophisticated form of segregation.

THE INFORMATION CONTROL
COMMISSION

This has rightly been called the information age. Vast quantities of information continue to pour out; there seems to be no end to it, or even a pause. Many feel that there is just too much of it, and something must be done. Was there no natural limit? Even as the oceans, the earth and the atmosphere can contain only so much toxic material, must there not only be a limit to the amount of information that can be jammed into our mental space? For some, the situation called to mind the garbage collectors' strike when heaps of refuse were everywhere; now, In the endless torrent of words, data, numbers and images there was much that is irrelevant, more that is repetitive to the point of plagiarism, and even more that is simply pointless. Libraries groan with their burdens, and even newsprint, a medium that is said to be atrophying in the digital age, is booming.

Given these conditions, it was inevitable that some regulatory measure would be enacted, although at first it had limited scope. Even then, the reception given to The Information Control Commission was mixed: while the need for such an agency was acknowledged, many saw it as the beginning of a period of rampant censorship. As a result, the Commission sought to distance itself as much as possible from out-and-out censorship. One result of this strategy was that in the beginning only new books in the most inconsequential literary genres were targeted for action at first. Confessionals, romance novels ("bodice busters"), and detective stories were on this list, followed, sometime later, by memoirs and self-published novels. Also included were those periodicals sold mainly at supermarket check-out stations in which the sex lives of celebrities were revealed.

But even here, simple censorship was avoided. Outright banning was never a consideration; instead, the Commission pursued what it called "soft regulation." Each copy of the publication was required to carry on its cover a prominent notice rating the amount of valid information it contained, in percentage terms, together with the reasons for that rating. As an example, a rating of 40% meant that only 40% of the book's contents consisted of valid information and was worthy of one's serious attention. Some speed readers took this provision as a personal challenge and accelerated their reading in accordance with the percentage. In their view, speed reading was a competitive event, and they were proud of the pace at which they turned pages, sprinting through those sections they deemed insignificant, and how quickly they could arrive at the end of the book. To them, reading was much like a track and field event, evaluated on the basis of distance covered and time elapsed.

Once the public had become accustomed to this initial program, the Commission extended it to include publications in all genres thereby broadening it immeasurably. While some grumbling was heard, as might be expected, it seemed as if the charge of censorship had been avoided. Some book reviewers, however, felt that the Commission was trespassing on their preserve, and often found a way to express their hostility in their reviews.

The agency was also active in publicizing its program, losing no opportunity to boast about the great number of man-hours saved that would otherwise have been spent bent over the printed page. This further antagonized the book reviewers, some of whom took to calling the agency's staff "non-librarians."

Having tightened the spigot on the publication of new books and publications, the Commission began the far more daunting job of reducing the quantity of materials already in existence. Under this program, great strides were made in lightening the shelves in many libraries, private as well as public. Individuals were offered generous payments in exchange for their collections, payments that did not constitute taxable income according to a special Internal Revenue Service ruling. This novel tax shelter proved to be effective, but was later abused as some canny individuals traded their rights to income from other sources for the library payments, thereby avoiding the tax. Once acquired, the Commission found it difficult to dispose of the vast amount of material that came pouring in. None of it could be burned since the awful memory of book burnings still festered in the consciousness of many. Instead, huge quantities were ground up in the jaws of giant machines located at secret sites scattered around the country. The resulting mulch proved to be surprisingly rich in nutrients, and, after re-packaging, was sold as plant food, helping, in a small way, to defray the expenses of the Commission.

All of its work so far having dealt with print media, the Commission now turned to Hollywood, radio and television where it sought to impose the same requirements. Considerable resistance was experienced when soap operas, to cite one instance, were forced to begin each episode with an announcement of the show's rating on the scale of valid information. Friction was also generated when historical re-creations, biographies and such programs were similarly evaluated. A particular firestorm broke out when the practice was extended to documentaries with results that raised many eyebrows. Some celebrity reputations were ruined.

A separate unit in the Commission was responsible for dealing with meaningless statistics. Those engaged in this work spent their days hunting for items like the following: "35.5% of those between 45 and 48 are occasionally unhappy," "66% of those canvassed were doubtful about the future," or "29% of women feel that one of their breasts is larger than the other." When these statistical nullities were identified, they were flagged and a footnote added so that the reader could appreciate their insignificance.

As the influence of the Commission grew, however, so did the number of its critics, not surprising in view of the repressive nature of its operations. Some headway in their efforts against the agency was made when the critics pointed out that its operations contributed, in no small measure, to the quantity of information it was designed to control. Against that criticism the Commission at first could do nothing but remain stoically silent since a response would further demonstrate its validity. In time, however, the continued growth in information reached such levels that the significance of the agency's contribution virtually disappeared.

THE NEGOTIABLE FIRE DEPARTMENT

There was a precedent for this agency, albeit one buried deep in history. Ancient Rome, in spite of its imperial glory, its Caesars, its mother tongue and its Colosseum spectacles, among other things, lacked an organized, public fire department. Into the breach stepped Marcus Vicinius Crassus, famed down the centuries for his wealth. Crassus employed a group of fire fighters who were, naturally, under his direction. When a fire broke out, Crassus' firemen raced to the scene where they assembled, waiting further directions. Nothing was done until Crassus arrived and negotiated an agreement with the desperate property owner as to how much Crassus would be paid for fighting the fire. The sums agreed to have not come down to us, but we might imagine the leverage Crassus applied as he bargained with the distraught property owner, the heat on their faces and the smoke in their nostrils, the flames rising higher and higher.

The modern descendants of Crassus' firefighters still exist here and there, usually in small towns and villages scattered across the countryside. Some have said that these groups first appeared in the Borscht Belt, that area about 100 miles northwest of New York City that once flourished as a summer resort for the City's Jewish population in the pre-air-conditioning era when their apartments became intolerable. But that was decades ago and the hotels and bungalow colonies once found there have since disappeared. During its decline it was often rumored that "Jewish lightning" had struck, an ironic reference to an act of arson by the property owner to collect on an insurance policy.

In the towns and villages that dotted this area there were usually volunteer fire departments. These usually consisted of a modest brick building with a siren and a well-polished fire truck. It was not uncommon to hear the screaming of the siren rising and falling and see one of the local businessmen—the butcher, perhaps—overweight and perspiring, his blood-stained apron flapping in the wind, sprinting to the firehouse to make it there before the fire engine pulled out. The firemen were an enthusiastic, but usually unsuccessful, bunch who did not lack a sense of humor. They were often heard to boast that they "never lost a foundation yet."

It may have been here in one of these Borscht Belt towns that the first bodies resembling Crassus' fire brigade appeared on the scene. In like fashion, they rushed to the fire and proceeded to negotiate the terms of their engagement. There were some important matters that had to be explored first: what was the market value of the property? how far had the fire advanced? how quickly, if at all, could the fire be contained? what would the property's market value be then? was there insurance? how much? how much would the fire department be paid? These were, typically, expedited negotiating sessions that ended with the payment of a good faith deposit and the signing of a memorandum of understanding, all accomplished with preternatural speed. In spite of that, some members of the brigade were occasionally known to stall negotiations with a view to buying the property later at a greatly reduced price. In time, some local lawyers, seeing an opportunity, offered their services, in a stand-by capacity (for a fee), to represent the property owner in the event of a fire. While this comforted the owners, it also lengthened the negotiations as the "Fire Lawyers," as they came to be known, tried to justify their fees.

It is not surprising that under these conditions these departments prospered in marked contrast with the dilapidated hotels and bungalow colonies and the general economic decline found throughout the area. While unemployment was very high and money scarce, the treasuries of these departments grew and grew. Faced with rising criticism, the agencies first pointed to their Roman model as if its antiquity would somehow validate their operation. When that failed, they argued that their activities merely spearheaded the advance of capitalism, suggesting, somehow, that in the absence of such an effort the opposition—Communism and state-ownership—might gain an advantage. Since this was a time when the Red Scare was still alive and a major concern, the contention seemed plausible.

But the very success of these operations proved to be a problem. Flush with cash, a condition with which they had little familiarity, the firemen spent lavishly on equipment, uniforms and buildings. The ordinary fire engine was traded in for a thing of beauty; streamlined and massive, it was big enough to house the whole company whereas the old vehicle required most of the men to hang along its sides as it raced to the fire. Uniforms were upgraded so that there were both summer and winter issues, although, to their credit, the departments decided against plumed helmets, thigh-high boots, and capes. Modesty was not to be found, however, when the old fire houses were demolished and replaced with more sumptuous buildings containing, besides the engine and fire-fighting equipment, a pool hall, a large dining room, a movie house and a roof garden designed as a German beer hall with barbecue facilities.

Such luxurious facilities could hardly be maintained while the surrounding area was growing poorer and poorer. In time, the disparity became intolerable, and the gaudy firehouses were demolished, the furnishings, the grand fire engine and all the other accoutrements of wealth were sold off, to be replaced by a prefabricated building of corrugated tin, and a used, economy model fire engine that had seen better days. The proceeds of this liquidation added further to the departments' treasuries, an unnatural situation that led, eventually, to the distribution of the surplus among the district's property owners and the imposition of a new set of reduced fees to be used on a mandatory basis in dealing with fires in the future. The glory days of the negotiable fire department were over.

THE INSPECTOR GENERAL FOR TV
COMMERCIALS

Originally a desk in an outlying part of the Federal Communications Commission, this office flowered together with the growth in television advertising. The seniors among us may remember the early days of TV when the screen was small, the image black, white, grainy and fluttering, programs were few and advertising unobtrusive. Since then the number of channels has multiplied and programs have proliferated, but advertising outpaced all of that and grew so disproportionately that it sometimes seemed to threaten the programs themselves.

The jurisdiction of this office is limited and does not include those programs devoted completely to advertising. Its mission, rather, is to deal with those commercials that appear at the beginning, during, and at the end of a program that purports to have some independent aesthetic or informational value. The IG is often heard to reminisce about how such commercials appeared rarely when TV was very young, how they grew in number over the years and how they long since became a problem requiring remedial attention. When he goes on in this way, of course, he is simply justifying his office, but most audience members nod in approval anyway.

The monitoring that is one of the office's basic activities was done physically at first. That is to say, a number of employees spent their days staring at the screen, each assigned to a specific channel, and making notes. That proved impractical as anybody could have predicted since it was not very long before these poor souls were burned out. To do nothing but watch TV all day long proved to be too much for the human constitution. Even when one, two, four, and, finally, six breaks were inserted in the work schedule the burden proved to be excessive. After a while every one of these workers broke down. Some became hysterical, others catatonic, and still others were led away babbling incoherently, tears running down their faces. Candid photos of some of these employees in distress somehow came into the possession of TIVO which used them effectively to promote its service as a way people could protect themselves against such dangers.

These employees were then replaced by computer programs whose electronic eyeballs were immune to such nervous break-downs. Once installed, they dutifully counted the number of commercials at each program break and sorted them into various categories. It should not have been a revelation, but most people were astonished to learn that, on average, 12 and sometimes even more separate commercial messages were railroaded through each break. And, when they were listed, most people were further astonished to see how unrelated these commercials were, both to each other and to the underlying program. If the viewer's half-attentive mind was looking for some common thread that bound them together, he need not have bothered: it did not exist.

This was where the Inspector General proposed a number of remedies. The first was a limitation on the number of commercials that could be aired at any one time, together with requirements as to the minimum and maximum lengths of each. Others addressed the character and appearance of the spokesman and even the pace at which he delivered his message. Once adopted, these changes had a positive effect. Many viewers agreed that the revised commercial breaks were less of a distraction from the program in which they had been inserted. The TV stations and advertisers, however, complained, the former of lost revenues and the latter of lost opportunities.

The IG's next proposal was much more radical—that there be some substantive common denominator shared by each of the commercials aired at a break. This meant, for example, that an ad for weight reduction could not appear at the same time as an ad for a car rental agency. There was some protest that this stricture violated the free speech guarantee of the federal constitution, but it never ripened into actual litigation. In time, this change had the effect of grouping related commercials at certain times. For example, from 7 to 8 p.m. became known as the financial hour when commercials involving annuities, mortgages, and banks were aired; the mid-afternoon hours, when many housewives watched soap operas, were filled with advertisements for cosmetics, new clothing fashions, feminine hygiene and cookware, and during the hours after midnight those suffering from insomnia could learn about superior mattresses and pillows and other remedies for their affliction.

Like some other public officials, the Inspector General proved to be too zealous in the discharge of his duties. He crossed the line, it developed, when he instituted a requirement that there be at least one 6 hour period a week that would be free of any commercial. The television stations and the advertising industry were outraged at first, but then reluctantly agreed when the requirement was modified so that the period need not be continuous but could be made up of one hour segments and aired when viewership was small. A different, and more violent reaction, however, came from a surprising quarter. Perhaps because of deeply-engrained habits, but possibly also for perverse reasons, the viewing public rejected this "pure" programming and demanded the restoration of commercials. This extraordinary development raised serious questions about the need for this agency, and, at least, about the scope of its jurisdiction. To the advertising industry, however, it was considered wonderful testimony in which countless viewers approved of their work, and, more particularly, of the entertainment value to be found in it. For them it was nothing less than confirmation of their basic metaphysical view, that there is nothing more important in the world than the buying and selling of goods and services.

THE EXTRA-TERRESTRIAL
TRAINING INSTITUTE

The message changed everything. Once a communication had been received from somewhere in the fathomless universe, and cleared, everyone's perspective changed radically. At first, however, the government maintained complete secrecy. Convinced that disclosure would produce mass chaos as the terrified masses would flee in all directions. Then, a carefully staged program was begun in which the possibility of extra-terrestrial life was increasingly discussed in the media followed by the appearance of authority figures who gradually concluded that it was likely. As a result, when the message became known there were only a few disturbances here and there.

The hard fact, however, was that we were not alone and alien beings were real, not merely the imaginings of science fiction writers. As the messages continued, experts worked long and hard to decipher them, and try to understand the nature of the beings that sent them and the world they inhabited. In time it became clear that the language used had three bases, number, geometric forms and shades of color, all combining to provide a means of expression that was complex, far-reaching and subtle, unlike anything on earth.

But another question occupied the minds of most people: were the aliens on the way to earth, and, if they were on the way, what were their intentions? In this state of affairs, many recalled science fiction stories they had read and movies they had seen, as well as episodes of "Star Trek" on television. It was in contemplation of these dramatic possibilities, unparalleled in the history of the world, that this Institute was created in order to prepare people for what would likely be the greatest cultural shock they would ever experience, and further communicate with the aliens. To a certain extent, those in the new body would be flying blind since nothing like the contemplated event had ever occurred. Given broad powers and generously funded, the agency was modeled, in part, on those military training centers that appear in wartimes. Like them, it sought to prepare large groups of people for extraordinary events, the precise nature of which could not be foreseen, as well as to enter into a dialogue with the extraterrestrials.

Once organized, the Institute launched two campaigns, both assuming that someday these beings would be here among us. In one, a variety of activities sought to strengthen and enlarge the individual's natural ability to empathize, whether with other humans or non-human beings, and even inanimate things. In the other, a series of re-enactments of historical events was undertaken, on the theory that some might prove to be useful preparation for the actual confrontation with aliens that awaited the world.

The premise of the first campaign was that empathy, as a faculty that exists in everyone to varying degrees, can be increased by training. In this light, it was said to be like a muscle that can be strengthened by repeated exercise over time. Its proponents pointed out how memory, a similar function, can be improved in this fashion, that a discipline known as "The Art of Memory," had existed for thousands of years, its practitioners sometimes achieving remarkable results, and that recently it had been suggested that the imagination could also be strengthened in a similar manner.

The empathy exercise, performed daily for one half hour, consisted, at first, in trying to project oneself into another person. At first, that other person was of the other gender. It came as no surprise that many men failed in the effort to cross the gender gap. For those who succeeded, the test was made more difficult by replacing ordinary humans as the targets with midgets, disabled people and others in costumes. Even later, the human targets were replaced by animals, at first, dogs and cats, then wild animals, then insects. These exercises, led by trained instructors, became popular, were often seen on television and were regularly discussed in newspapers and on the internet. To a certain extent, they replaced a variety of group activities including calisthenics, tai chi, and yoga, but on a much larger scale.

As to the second approach, it was observed that historical re-enactments had existed for a long time. although they had never amounted to more than a marginal activity engaged in by some hobbyists for their amusement. Chief among these were the Civil War re-enactments in which men regularly dressed themselves as combatants on both sides, camped at historical sites, and simulated the actual battles. The devotion of the Civil War enthusiasts to detail was impressive although their numbers were not great. There were also those who re-enacted events of the Revolutionary War, although they were even fewer in number.

Using these scattered groups as models, the agency began to organize historical re-enactments of other events that, because of the dramatic differences between the groups involved, might evoke the confrontation that was yet to come between humanity and the aliens.

Among the first were the meetings between the Spanish forces of Cortez and the Aztecs, Pizarro and the Incas, and between the Dutch explorers and the Indians who lived in what is now New York City. While the cultural disparity between the two groups in each case was great, it paled when compared with that involving humanity and the aliens. Well-intentioned as they were, these events rarely achieved anything more serious than an occasional diversion for those looking for a little novelty.

Amid the uncertainty, and with growing fears that the extra-terrestrials were getting ready to attack, a national emergency was declared. Many countries put themselves on a war footing, armies were assembled, military stockpiles checked and citizen advisories were frequently broadcast. Later, curfews were ordered, and lights had to be turned off by 9 p.m. The night-time scene of New York City under these conditions was both eerie and beautiful.

In this state of affairs, some public commentators reached into the past and resurrected H. G. Wells' "The War of the Worlds." That story, and the radio dramatization on which it was based, in which aliens suddenly appeared and began destroying humanity seemed frighteningly applicable, notwithstanding the fact that the invaders in the story quickly die off because they lacked immunity from microorganisms found in human bodies. Not least signifi-cant was the source of the Wells' story. Upon hearing an account of the conquest of Tasmania and the systematic slaughter of its natives, Wells was drawn to imagine what such a catastrophic event would be like from the point of view of the victims, and, moreover, if the hostile forces were, not European colonizers, but extra-terrestrial beings. As relevant as Wells' story seemed, how-ever, it offered little comfort. With uncertainty threatening to produce panic, it did little good to think that the aliens would be no match for the bugs that had been developed in our bodies over countless generations.

When the message had finally been deciphered, a response seemed in order, but there was a considerable division of opinion as to what it should be. While some suggested a peaceful tone, others were aggressive, and still others argued for silence. The question was political in nature, but historical as well, and complicated by our ignorance of the psychology of those who sent the message. Ultimately, after lengthy and intense debate, it was decided to enter into a cautious dialogue with the aliens in the hope of learning more about them and their intentions.

As that dialogue proceeded, it effectively pushed to the side anything else that might have qualified as news. Every night at 7, the world listened closely as the most recent installment was replayed and then subjected to critical analysis by various experts. Gradually, two bodies of information began to take shape from these talks. The first consisted largely of a history of humanity on earth that was transmitted to the aliens as our spokesman tried to explain who we are, how we function, what we have done, and what we hope to do in the future. For many, this was fascinating in itself; it was as if the species at large had paraded before a vast mirror. The second was a rudimentary description of the aliens gleaned from the ongoing dialogue. Almost from the beginning, it was apparent that we were dealing with superior beings and a culture far more advanced than ours. While a certain portion of the information from the aliens could not be understood even by the best de-coding experts, it eventually became clear that the relationship between our species and theirs could most appropriately be described in terms of that existing between us and our pet cats and dogs. That conclusion proved to be insufferable to most of us since it spoke of our inferiority. In one stroke, our world had been turned upside down; where we once took pride in being the dominant species, we now found ourselves members of a lower class (more exactly, a lower species), deprived of many powers and rights. Just how far we had been demoted remained to be seen. Some argued that we had become like the Untouchables in the caste system in India, but others claimed that our demotion was even greater than that.

As we continued to struggle to accommodate the new reality, some advantages appeared. The usual preoccupation with foreign affairs soon faded. Disputes over territory, for example, seemed pointless now that all of humanity had been crowded together into one small place in the universe, and shown to be virtually powerless in relation to the aliens. That proved to be a beneficial development as humanity devoted less and less time and energy to applauding itself and waging internecine warfare.

Little attention had been given, however, to the age of the communication, that is, when it had been transmitted. The common impression was that what had been received was like a call from another room in one's home. Most people were startled to learn that the message had been traveling through space for countless light years having been sent before our remotest ancestors crawled out of the ocean ... no! even before the earth and its oceans had been formed; much, much earlier. How could there be such foresight? What did it mean? Furthermore, our response (if and when it was made) would have to travel the same incredible distance over the same incredible time period before it was received at the other end. Would there be anyone there after such a period of time? And deep in the future, would anyone there even remember that a conversation had been initiated? Would anyone even remember that a conversation had been struck up? Or were those who called to us immortal? Such thoughts humbled even the most resolute and self-assured of individuals, making plain how brief and inconsequential is the life of man.

In view of these circumstances, the foresight of those beings who sent the messages seemed even more astonishing. How was it done? The gulf between humanity and the extra-terrestrials seemed to grow ever greater. Many began to think of the aliens as gods, a development that was especially remarkable since religion had been in decline for many years. Attendance at houses of worship had fallen off dramatically and religious utterances—even religious thinking—had diminished to the point where some social critics began talking of an Age of Atheism.

This new religious development had the further effect of weakening the Institute's foundation. To the extent extra-terrestrials had been deified they had been removed from human affairs and placed with the gods in a distant heaven. With this change in public opinion it was inevitable that the Institute's funding would be reduced, and the agency, having atrophied, was rarely mentioned in the media.

THE HOUSEHOLD BUDGET OFFICE

The chorus of complaints that greeted the new governmental regulation of household budgets was hardly a surprise: this was still another intrusion by the state into private life. But something had to be done. With an economy that had been struggling for years, shocking unemployment, more and more bankruptcies, and the growing numbers of people who lived alone, help was needed. Congress responded by creating this new agency that effectively drew up a chair for the federal government at that kitchen table where the typical family sits down to prepare the household budget.

One of the main features of the new law was the requirement that every household file a budget every year. That the filing date was April 15th seemed only natural given the relationship between budgeting and the taxation of income. But that was not the only characteristic the budget and tax systems had in common. Both were said to be "voluntary," although everyone knew that that was a euphemism, since participation in both was mandatory and there were penalties for non-compliance. Furthermore, half of the budget covered substantially the same ground as the tax filing—income—although the one was prospective and the other retrospective.

Once established, the Office moved quickly to develop and distribute appropriate forms, here, too, following the lead of the tax system. Again, complaints were heard—the forms were confusing, the instructions were ambiguous, there was no point to it, etc. Training in the preparation of a budget also began. Free courses were given around the country, usually at local YMCAs, and in high schools the standard courses in home economics were revised to include the new subject of budgeting. New emigrants seeking citizenship as well as those who had gone through bankruptcy, were required to take these courses. Many who took them felt as if they were struggling to learn a foreign language, so lacking in financial planning had their lives been and so strange were the words and ideas they encountered.

Once filed, the budget became a significant influence in the individual's life, the source of some significant behavior modification. Since actual expenditures were not to exceed the budgeted amounts, one had to keep these limits continually in mind. In the event of transgressions, penalties were incurred. For the first infractions fines were imposed; if other violations followed, the penalties became more severe. When items of income actually received varied from estimates, an amendment was necessary.

Once the budget was filed, the emphasis shifted to its administration. Here, again, many found it difficult to reconcile themselves with the document's strictures; this was especially the case for those on limited incomes. To deal with these problems, Office representatives worked closely with individuals, usually at their homes. During these consultations the budget was reviewed and the individual's financial affairs and household subjected to rigorous examination. Closets, drawers, cabinets, and even refrigerators were scrutinized. In the search for wasteful behavior that could be corrected, there seemed nothing that was too small or insignificant. For example, Office representatives with homeowners in tow, tramped into the bathroom where the position of the roll of toilet paper in its receptacle was examined. Lengthy studies in the Office had established convincingly that a toilet paper roll unrolled from the top would last longer than if it was unrolled from the bottom. Although the actual difference in cost in the overall operation of a household might be small, and not even aggregate much over the years, the Office liked to focus on this matter whenever possible, believing it had a powerful symbolic value and could be persuasive in modifying the individual's overall behavior. In lecturing the aberrant homeowner on the subject, The Office representative tended to talk about it as if it had extraordinary significance, and that the entire population could be divided into two camps on that basis: the Abovists and the Belowists.

A small matter, they went on, but they had determined that Abovists were usually outgoing, friendly and spent freely, while Belowists were usually shy, introspective and frugal.

Most of these home visits proved successful in correcting budget problems, but there remained cases that were intransigent and called for further action. Towards that end, an Office representative was assigned to accompany the individual whenever he or she went shopping. Among other things, the representative discouraged the shopper from making impulse purchases, steered him or her away from more expensive stores and pricey items and towards those on sale or that could be bought at discount in volume. These actions were generally effective, but even then there remained some hard cases that called for even more extreme measures. Exercising some of the extraordinary powers it had been granted by the enabling legislation, the Office cancelled the individual's credit cards, and set up a system of oversight regulation with respect to any future purchases of goods or services. Notices were published in the media and on the web and sent directly to local vendors advising them that these individuals were subject to restrictions and could not make purchases without producing the appropriate documentation detailing what could be bought, in what amounts, and at what prices. Failure to comply resulted in substantial penalties. To some it seemed like the rationing system that had been put in place during World War II. But the arrangement was not without obloquy. News of the imposition of such restrictions inevitably got out in the neighborhood to the shame of the individual affected. He or she effectively became a second class citizen.

Over the years the Office issued more and more regulations governing the making and administration of the household budget. As the regulatory framework grew in complexity, practitioners began to appear who specialized in this kind of work, and offered to assist the householder for a fee. In a manner reminiscent of that in which more and more taxpayers threw up their hands after struggling with the tax forms and hired professionals to prepare their returns, these budget experts were called on more and more often to prepare budgets and represent individuals in their dealings with the Household Budget Office. In time, these operators formed an organization that established standards to be observed in their work and certified compliance with them. Thereafter, those who satisfied the requirements were able to represent themselves as "Certified Budget Analysts," or "CBAs," a title that might secure by similarity some of the social cachet of Certified Public Accountant or CPAs. A few of these practitioners created inter-active websites that did well, and one was said to be negotiating a deal with a publisher for a book entitled "The Idiot's Guide to Household Budgeting."

In another development that suggested the Office was following the lead of the Internal Revenue Service, the Office began to prosecute one or two celebrities during the filing season every year for failure to comply with its requirements in the belief that such showcase trials would encourage compliance. Over the years those who found themselves publicly embarrassed in this fashion included the right fielder for the New York Yankees, a Hollywood starlet, and, most notoriously, an Assistant Secretary in the Internal Revenue Service. In spite of these measures, however, a considerable number of citizens failed to submit the required paperwork, continuing to operate in what the Office referred to, disparagingly, as "underground budgeting."

THE BUREAU OF NOMENCLATURE

This agency's function has long roots reaching back to Adam in the Bible who named the animals as they passed before him, and, more recently, Linnaeus, the 18th Century Swedish naturalist who created the binomial nomenclature by which living things are now known. But naming is significant for more than its long history, being the first step in comprehending something, whether that thing is as small as an insect, or as large as a galaxy. Once a subject's name has been attached, the doors of understanding swing open and its nature is ready to be revealed.

Notwithstanding that significance, the selection of a name has often been a random affair. Consider the names that we carry throughout our lives. The surname we inherit may derive from our ancestors' occupation ("Smith," "Farmer"), or where they lived ("deGaulle"). The choice of a personal name may be motivated by a desire to remember a relative or an admired person. Personal naming has also been a rather casual affair, free of official sanctions. Even the mandatory birth certificate does not require that a personal name be affixed to the new-born, and thereafter one might change his name without much difficulty at least until the advent of this agency which thereafter regulated such matters. But, of course, personal naming is just one part of the field of nomenclature, a fact reflected in the broad jurisdiction given to this Bureau. Perhaps of greater significance may be the naming of such items as places, and events, a procedure where custom dictates that the discoverer's name be assigned to that newly found as a kind of reward. Consider, for example, Parkinson's, Hodgkin's, and

Alzheimer's diseases in the medical field and the Hudson River and the Americas in geography.

When this Bureau was organized and began functioning it was so well-received that many wondered how the world could have gotten along so long without it. Very soon it became a central clearing house for names and none could have legal effect unless it had been registered with this here. By enforcing this requirement over the years the agency was able to clear up a great deal of confusion and ambiguity with respect to personal names. Aliases and nicknames were discouraged and the practice of naming progeny with roman numerals was curtailed.

But it was in the world of commerce that the Bureau had its greatest impact. Among its first clients was a Korean car maker drawn, in part, by unfamiliarity with the subtleties of American English and the realization that a misstep here could be fatal. Perhaps their advisers also told them the cautionary tale of the Edsel, a car name that long ago became synonymous with failure, its pudendum shaped grill a matter of ribald humor. There had been other disasters in this field, including the time when another car manufacturer, drawn to birds' names because of the flight, speed, grace and maneuverability of those creatures, decided to call one model the "Pelican." While that bird is wonderful in the air, it is something less than that on the ground, where it waddles about like a grumpy old man with a massive double chin. Disappointing sales of that model led the manufacturer to conduct a series of polls that indicated the name alone dissuaded some people from buying the car. Unwilling to give up ornithology, however, the firm turned to the raptors and decided that a new model should be called "The Osprey," a name that proved to be rather ambiguous to many people and had little effect on sales..

In the scope of the Bureau's commercial operations, however, cars did not bulk large; by far the greatest part of its efforts was devoted to pharmaceuticals. The list of these products was long because each drug had three names—the chemical name, the product name, and the generic name. It was only of minor assistance in sorting through them that the product name had an initial capital letter and the generic name did not. Because there was such a multitude of items to be named in this field, the Bureau's staff often became hard-pressed. After drawing many names from the classical world, and a number of other sources, they found themselves using acronyms, neologisms, and words with numbers.

Other subjects that required naming were hotels, gated communities, consumer products, and even new fruits and vegetables. The field of consumer products alone was large including refrigerators, wristwatches and clothing lines, to name a few, and, since the introduction of a new model usually required a new name, the field was always expanding.

The Bureau's staff liked to call themselves "Designators," and were mindful of the traditional aspects of their work, although they sometimes indulged a taste for innovation. So, for example, hotel names usually evoked wealth—mansions or palaces—and gated communities usually evoked idyllic beaches or landscapes. In their wide-ranging deliberations the Designators were often called upon to ponder the suitability of names for plants and animals, the use of acronyms, word-number combinations and foreign words and phrases. With regard to the last, French and Italian appeared from time to time, German, Dutch and Russian rarely, if ever. The Designators often observed that a good name is like a good metaphor in that there should be a significant sharing of characteristics. By this reasoning, for example, a car make could be a Jaguar, but not a camel, hippo or a walrus; a car model might be a Malibu or a Sedona, but not a Bronx or a Flatbush; a jeweled pendant might be a starburst, but not a spadeful. Designators were often heard to talk about the importance of fads, and how easily and quickly public opinion could change. In this vein, they took all of naming as their province, and, so inspired, would go on at some length about the names of actors and actresses: how Archibald Leach became Cary Grant, Issur Demsky became Kirk Douglas, and Natalia Nikolaevna Zebharenko became Natalie Wood. But then public opinion changed, and where awkward ethnic names had been rejected, they now were in style, as witness the case of Zack Galifanakis. It was an interesting exercise about the vagaries of naming, but not relevant to the Bureau's commercial work which was the naming of products and services—except in one respect. In each case, duplication had to be avoided. Just as the name "Cary Grant" could be used only once, the name "Focus," attached to a certain model Ford, could not be given to a Buick. To avoid the problem, it was necessary to maintain a register of the names used for products and services and consulting this register was always the last step in the work of the Designators.

The Designators also believed that naming was an art and they insisted they were artists in every sense of the word. Just as the art of painting evolved in many directions, with many specialties, so, too, did the art of naming. Among the Designators there were those who worked the biosphere, deriving names from flora and fauna. Then there were those who specialized in acronyms;

others in foreign languages, still others in abbreviations, yet others in portmanteau words. Even beyond those, there were some—and they believed themselves the purest of all—who specialized in names that had never been seen before, but were made up, so to speak, out of whole cloth.

While it was popularly believed that the Designators simply waited around for inspiration to strike, the truth was that they relied on modern tools both in choosing a name and evaluating both its suitability and effectiveness. Market analysis and polling were always used in testing the acceptability of new names, as well as crowd sourcing. In time, the Bureau was able to compile a considerable record of successful naming of which it was very proud.

Although the bulk of its work was commercial, the agency also provided certain consulting services for individuals. These included new parents who sought advice on personal names for their children, and emigrants who realized that in trying to fit into a new and different society their family names might be impediments because they were difficult to pronounce or suggested an ethnicity in disfavor. In such cases the Designators felt that they performed valuable services in helping the new citizens become integrated into society. For this purpose the Bureau kept statistics showing the number of people bearing a certain name and their percentage in the population as well as possible alternatives. Some of those unhappy with their given names applied to the Bureau for the purpose of hyphenating their last name, or adding an ornamental "de" or "von." There were even some who sought to add a Roman numeral to their names even when an actual basis for that was lacking. In general, however, those applications were denied.

Among the most curious of the Bureau's functions was its advice to those seeking a completely new name. Here its work consisted of a lengthy analysis of the individual in order to understand his background, characteristics, foibles, preferences and aversions. Once that was complete, the search began for that single word or phrase that would best express his identity. There were few guides available for such daunting, unusual work, but, to the astonishment of many, it turned out that Damon Runyon's "Guys and Dolls," a novel, which became a musical and a film, was one. As some may recall, Runyon had a genius for creating names that seemed to capture the essence of his characters. Examples included Sky Masterson, named for his willingness to bet, The Lemon Drop Kid, named for his sweet tooth, and Regret, named for the emotion with which he usually left the race track.

OFFICE OF TAX COMPLEXITY

Enactment of the legislation creating this office by amendment to the Internal Revenue Code was largely due to the concerted efforts of certified public accountants, H&R Block, Hewitt Jackson and similar firms. Their successful lobbying had some unexpected results. The days when individuals would labor over their tax returns passed into history where they joined those who cut wood for the fireplace and forked hay in the stables. Now, no one would think of doing his or her own return; it would have been madness.

Positions in the new office were mainly filled by those who had developed their skills in various Congressional offices where they learned how to create a rider to a measure sufficiently incomprehensible to pass muster in a heated debate, but comprehensible enough to a calm, experienced judge before whom it was later brought for review. It was not a difficult transition in most cases.

The theory of tax complexity was not itself that abstruse. To the extent that the taxpayer's obligation could be increased, the government's aggregate revenues would also increase, and that increase would be more acceptable if the underlying provision was as obscure as possible. Those who fully grasped this theory tended to explain it in terms of its diametric opposite. A single, flat income tax, universally understood and simple to administer would provide none of the ambiguity and confusion that any seasoned tax collector could exploit in order to increase the yield, and therefore would be less productive.

The Office of Tax Complexity had final approval over all tax proposals developed by component divisions of the Internal Revenue Service. In reviewing and modifying many of the provisions that came before it they used some of the following techniques:

Extended incorporation by reference. Incorporation by reference usually directs the reader away from the page he is studying to another page containing the relevant material. This simple step was multiplied by the Office, requiring the reader to go on to a third page, and, sometimes, even further, to a fourth page. In such cases, the hapless reader was often seen trying to keep as many as four books open to the right pages with fingers, elbows, pens and whatever else was handy. It could be a remarkable balancing act. If he was reading on a computer monitor, the procedure could be even more difficult.

Ambiguous paragraphing. Not only was the text broken up into the smallest possible paragraphs, the designation of those parts itself became a fertile field for complication. For example, a basic provision might be numbered 437. The first group of subdivisions would have capital letters, the next group numbered with Latin numbers, the following group lower case letters, the arrangement then re-started with appropriate indentations. Run-on sentences were common and the rules of grammar were regularly ignored. Semicolons were used frequently since there was abundant psychological evidence that most people are confused about the proper use and meaning of that punctuation mark.

Footnote misdirection. While the traditional role of the footnote is to supplement or clarify a provision in the main text, here the roles were reversed and the main point was to be found, not in the main text, but in the footnote. As if this was not confusing enough, the creators of this strategy reduced the type size used in the footnotes to make them even more difficult to read.

Repealed provisions. From time to time the Office resurrected a repealed provision and included it among those now in effect, albeit with a very small footnote indicating that it was no longer in effect. In its defense, the Office argued that although the provision was not now in effect, it had been in effect at one time and there would always be taxpayers who, perhaps for failure to pay their taxes during that prior period, must now compute their tax liability using that provision. The responsive argument that there would be very few who fell into this category, fell on deaf ears. Some tax advisors called these "Frankenstein Provisions."

Foreign words and phrases. Since Latinisms had already secured a place in the financial sphere, it was not difficult to add to those already in use others certain to be misunderstood or ignored. How should the taxpayer respond, for example, to the phrase "ad astra per ardua," when included with instructions for paying the tax due? The introduction of an occasional French or German word or phrase also proved to be effective, even to native speakers of those languages for they were usually inappropriate.

Even in the matter of the common index or occasional glossary small changes could produce the desired effect. These might take the form of an omission or a re-definition capable of leading the taxpayer further astray, adding to the frustration that would inevitably drive him or her into the arms of the professional tax preparer.

A similar dynamic was frequently used in the examples offered to explain more difficult provisions. The simple events used formerly were replaced by anecdotes filled with exotic details of questionable relevance. The taxpayer in one such example was described as a veteran auctioneer suffering from agoraphobia, a condition explored at some length. In another example the taxpayer was a divorced woman struggling to raise teen-age sons who had criminal proclivities. In yet a third example a capital asset referred to as a forgery of an Andrea del Sarto masterpiece, the forgery described at some length.

The forms required to determine and report one's tax were not exempt from this effort to complicate matters. Where one form had been in use, it was now broken down into two or more. Schedules were also multiplied and the taxpayer referred from one form and schedule to others for little reason other than to generate the possibility of confusion that always accompanies incorporation by reference.

The cumulative effect of these techniques was to make the body of tax regulations broader, deeper and more difficult to comprehend. In some scholarly quarters discussions on some of the provisions began to take on the shape of the endless disputation characteristic of Talmudic analysis, biblical exegesis or moral casuistry. At conventions and other gatherings some regulations were subject to endless analysis and discussion, not for the purpose of reducing a tax bill, but simply to penetrate to the heart of a text that had become so byzantine it threatened to pass beyond all human understanding.

Inevitably, many issues relating to these problematic provisions landed in the special tax court established to hear these matters. Although committed to judicial fairness, this body often acted as if it was only interested in producing more tax revenue. How, then, might one explain the procedure in that forum that dictates not only that the burden of proof is on the petitioner seeking relief, but that he is presumed to be wrong?

THE OBESITY POLICE DEPARTMENT

The time had come for action. What was at first a statistic, had grown over the years into a scandal, a matter of national concern and then an emergency. Overweight men and women and even children were everywhere; it seemed as if they constituted a separate species—homo grosso—capable of speedier reproduction than their genetic cousins. You could see them waddling about on the sidewalks and other public places, making them even more crowded than they had been. On buses and in trains and subways the obese regularly sprawled over two seats forcing others to stand. They could negotiate turnstiles only with an adroit maneuver, something like a pirouette. Even the fashion industry, traditionally the province of the gaunt model near starvation, seemed to fall into place, using heavier men and women in an effort to appeal to the typical consumer.

Attempts to deal with the problem took a number of forms. The medical profession talked incessantly about the health risks associated with being overweight. The grim face of the U.S. Surgeon General was seen frequently issuing stern warnings. Public service announcements appeared on television and in the print media. Monthly contests were held with substantial prizes awarded to those who succeeded in losing the most poundage or the biggest percentage of their weight. In lunch rooms, restaurants and cafeterias menus were revised over and over in an effort to reduce caloric intake and slow the processing of food into bodily fat. Sweet drinks, already regulated, were now banned. But these and other steps failed to slow what was now being called an epidemic.

It was not as if no one was aware of the evolutionary basis of obesity. Over countless centuries our primitive forebears were so shaped by the dangers and uncertainty surrounding them that they became programmed to eat food rapidly and in large amounts. Such an adaptation might have been vital for survival in an age when the sabre-toothed tiger could have been on your back if you paused to think about your food, but in today's world restaurants are usually only steps away and the refrigerator is even closer. Combining this adaptation and the easy availability of food is a recipe for obesity.

The first efforts to use law-enforcement techniques to curb obesity were made by localities where the situation had become egregious. Laws were enacted making obesity an offense and creating enforcement machinery. Legislative attention around the country was focused on the experiment, and, although the results were mixed, many an official found in them a warrant to proceed.

The typical program had two parts: a police force and a judiciary. The police wore special uniforms and insignia to make it easy to identify them and avoid mistaking them for other police. A combination of good pay and benefits and a certain romance associated with the position made them desirable positions. There was a catch, however: the Obese Police could not be obese themselves. Those who did become overweight were summarily discharged.

The powers of these police were limited to obesity offenses. Most of the members walked a beat, and, at least in the beginning, simply sized up those who came into view, proceeding further only in those cases where the subject seemed overweight. Probable cause for obesity, as this concept came to be known, was to be productive of a great deal of litigation. Equipped with a compact scale, a measuring device, and a handy guide, the officer quickly developed the relevant data, and, if it exceeded certain limits set forth in the guide, issued a ticket for violation of the Obesity Act. To some degree it was like the action taken when a policeman suspects a car driver of being intoxicated, especially after new technological devices, not unlike breathalyzers, were put into use by the Obesity Police.

The ticket constituted both notice of a violation of the law and of a fine due if the incident was a first offense. For repeat offenders, or if the fine was not paid, a summons to appear in court was issued. The court in question had a limited jurisdiction confined to cases involving obesity. While most of the respondents represented themselves, a small number of lawyers specializing in such matters were always at hand to assit, for a fee (the "Fat Bar"). At the hearing the respondent was presumed guilty (overweight), and he or she was required to persuade the judge otherwise. Among the defenses offered there was a flat-out denial of the computation, incorrect adjustments for age, sex or ethnicity, the scale used had not been certified as to its accuracy, and the bodily weight alleged failed to adjust for heavy items being carried or worn.

Upon a determination of guilt, the judge then turned to the penalty phase of the proceedings. While he had considerable discretion here, the overall goal was the reduction in weight of the obese respondent and his eventual return to society slimmed down. Among the remedies frequently used were mandatory exercise programs, dieting regiments, refrigerators with timed locks, and counseling. Those who went for counseling were taught the latest in cognitive behavior techniques. Sometimes, the individual's access to TV was prohibited to change sedentary eating habits while viewing the screen. In more extreme cases, he or she was forced out of doors whether at home or at work according to a schedule. These directives were not self-executing, of course, and the obese individual could not be counted on to carry them out by himself or herself. This is where the ancillary functions of the Obesity Police came in to play. Those assigned to such duty supervised the weight-reduction activities both in public and in the privacy of the individual's home. The Police Officers so occupied could often be seen going from door to door and making appropriate hourly entries in their journals as reuired by their job manual. Inside, the Officer inspected the contents of the refrigerator and cupboards, confiscating snack foods and other items that were inconsistent with a slim figure.

Obesity Police work was not completely lacking in the excitement and risk-taking characteristic of the work of some of their law enforcement brothers and sisters. A special plainclothes unit in the Department carried out surprise raids on all-you-can-eat buffet restaurants. The legal basis for such operations was that these businesses aided and abetted in the creation of criminal obesity. The raids by these flying squads often resulted in the apprehension of obese customers caught in the act. These raids were not simple matters since these buffets sprang up unannounced and in unlikely places. In some ways they were like the impromptu and secret drinking places that popped up overnight during Prohibition. Passwords were required and their locations could only be known through word of mouth since they were never advertised.

Obesity Police work was not without some opportunity for special rewards. Medals were awarded for extraordinary accomplishments in the field of obesity control, both individually and in the aggregate, and service stripes were worn proudly for years devoted to this essential service. Most members of the Department felt strongly that they were doing meaningful work that contributed to national security and well-being. At Police Headquarters there were photos and paraphernalia attesting to heroic acts and length of service. The grim expression on the faces in these photos bore witness to the seriousness with which they carried out their important work.

For repeat offenders of the obesity laws, remedial action sometimes took a harsher form. Depending on the weight involved, earlier offenses, and other relevant factors, the obese individual might find himself in police custody, on his way to a spa that functioned essentially like a basic training camp for those drafted into the army. Beyond even that, there were a few measures so extreme that one trembles just thinking about them. Let it be sufficient to say that mandatory fasting and even surgery were in this category. Unforgettable were those moments on the late TV news showing an operating room (how did they ever film it?) with a grossly overweight woman held down by a number of grim nurses while a team of surgeons performed a gastric by-pass procedure on the unwilling patient. For those who looked away, the stentorian tones of the commentator left no doubt as to the moral message.

With the waning of prosperity and the coming of harder times obesity began to fade. It was almost as if the stock market decline had been synchronized with weight loss and the Dow Jones

Industrial Average was moving in tandem with the average citizen's weight. In retrospect, it was seen that prosperity meant obesity. Even to the casual observer the legions of the roly-poly seemed to have been decimated. That change, of course, drew into question the need for the Obesity Police. With retirements, transfers and buy-outs, the force gradually shrank and it was not long before it passed away, leaving only memories of constabulary glory.

THE PREDICTION REVIEW COMMISSION

The business of predicting the future has had a poor reputation until recently; just to name some of its practitioners suggests their involvement in the black arts: fortune-tellers, clairvoyants, crystal ball gazers, tea leave readers, seers, oracles and prophesiers. Only in the modern era has this activity become respectable; employing scientific and technological methods, it now occupies a larger role in daily life. Forecasting the weather may have been a bellwether in this change, but as we became so much more mobile, we also grew familiar with such ideas as estimated time of travel and the projected clock hour of our arrival. In these and other circumstances it is possible to see how we are increasingly tilted toward the future. It could even be argued that much of progress is marked by improvements in forecasting the future.

As predictions became more common, especially in the world of commerce, it was soon plain that some sort of regulation was needed, leading, eventually, to the creation of this governmental body. The new commission was empowered to record all public prognostications, weigh their probability, and, ex post facto, determine to what extent they came true. The recording alone had a sobering effect on many who made predictions. Knowing that such claims would not simply disappear into the air and be forgotten, but would become part of the public record, caused many to pause and reflect, and some actually to desist from making them.

Once recorded, the prediction was sent to the appropriate department within the Commission for closer analysis by experts in the field. Here the inquiry concerned such matters as plausibility, the period of time in which the predicted event was expected to occur, and the commercial and/or political significance of that occurrence. Finally, the probability of occurrence was calculated and published weekly. Since that probability was expressed in the form of odds, these statements automatically took on the allure usually associated with racetrack betting and summoned up images of horses thundering around the bend, their jockeys whipping them on to the finish line. It was inevitable, therefore, that these statements would generate a great deal of wagering activity.

The tracking of these predictions, however, often proved to be difficult. Among other things, some time frame in which the event forecast was to come true had to be chosen. More than a few decisions by the Commission as to the occurrences were challenged on the ground that they were premature, the events predicted not yet having had a chance to ripen into reality.

In time, the Commission developed a substantial file of predictions. As part of a program to heighten awareness of its work, the Commission began publishing a list of 10 new predictions every week together with the odds that they would come true. These predictions covered a broad variety of activities. The result of a sporting event was used from time to time; others were a designated weather event, the outcome of an election, and the rise or fall of the Dow Jones Industrial Average. In compiling these groups the Commission sought to achieve a balance with respect to the periods of time within which the predictions could reasonably be expected to occur. So, for example, a typical group might include a prediction about the results of next Saturday's football game, a prediction about which party would gain control in Congress in the next election, and a prediction about whether New Orleans would become the site of the 2020 Olympic Games.

It was not long after the appearance of the list of 10 predictions that a group of smart operators began to apply crowdsourcing to them. This development may have had its roots in the polling that some major advertisers undertook from time to time as part of their market research. Since the polling arrangement was already in place, it was a simple matter to add to the list of prepared questions a few more relating to the 10 predictions. At first, this seemed foolish to some, but it turned out otherwise. The crowd proved to be more accurate than almost all individuals in weighing the likelihood of the predicted events coming true. Encouraged by this experience, the Commission increased the size of the crowd on the theory that there was a direct relationship between its size and the accuracy of its predictions.

The larger goal of the agency, however, was to show the public that the field of predicting was broad and varied, ranging from conservative statements almost certain to come true, to those fantastic claims equally certain never to happen. It was hoped that this kind of analysis would better equip the ordinary individual in making sense of predictions. Studies by the Commission had demonstrated that the ability to foretell events varies considerably from person to person involving an intricate balancing of knowledge, recollections and judgment. At one extreme are those unable to see very far ahead at all; at the other, those with an extraordinary power to discern the future. It was hoped that with appropriate training and exercise this faculty could be strengthened. This turned out to be an ambitious program seeking nothing less than a grounding in the rational of one's anticipation of the future.

Separate and apart from these activities, the Commission kept a record of the author of each public prediction and its success or failure. In this connection a rating system was created that became widely used in the field of forecasting. A "Prediction Quotient" (or "PQ," as it came to be known) concisely expressed the subject's overall success or failure in foretelling the future. In an attempt to gain for it some instant credibility, it was calibrated like the well-known Intelligence Quotient. As an example, where an IQ of 150 signified intellectual brilliance, a PQ of the same number would signify brilliance in futuristics. Those with a very high PQ found themselves celebrities pursued wherever they went by crowds hoping to learn of the future. This celebrity was usually short-lived, however, for it was not long before these individuals erred in predicting what lay ahead, whether that involved the stock market, global warming, or one's love life. In this the Commission usually played a part for it was especially attentive to the forecasts of these celebrities and diligent in publicizing them, as part of its overall policy of making predictions as realistic as possible.

In the political sphere the PQ of a candidate could often be the crucial element in an election campaign; without a satisfactory rating, the candidate would seem unqualified. Those who secured an office, whether by election or appointment, were also careful to maintain an acceptable PQ. Unfortunately, the best way to do this was by confining one's public utterances to the most meaningless of generalities and avoiding at all costs anything that suggested a specific view of the future. This led to political debates and prime time interviews in which the audience was left scratching its collective head for failure to understand anything that had been said.

While the agency's original mandate was to operate only with respect to public discourse, it was not long before its operations were felt with respect to private conversations as well. Since even small talk is replete with predictions, it, too, began to be scrutinized. Most people were surprised to learn that so much of what they say is oriented to the future, and, subsequently, found themselves pausing before dashing off such innocent remarks as "Hope to see you soon," "Have a nice day," or "Tomorrow I'm jammed. How about Wednesday?" Increasingly, people felt pressed to abjure the future and live in the present. In time these changes were felt in other areas. Promissory statements, now seen as joining a prediction and an obligation, were seen in a new light, as was planning for the future, in general. Daydreaming, a pastime to which everyone devotes some time, was recognized as having a predictive character and a conscious effort was made to avoid it. And who was the apostle of this attitude, the enemy of prediction? Why, none other than St. Matthew who memorably directs us to "Take.... no thought for the morrow: for the morrow shall take thought for the things of itself. Sufficient unto the day is the evil thereof."

Was all this change a good thing? Some critics argued that it was unnatural and tended to suppress the imagination. To the extent the individual was discouraged from thinking about the future, he became mired in the present and blind to the consequences of his decisions. In short, it signaled the end of progress.

Aware of this criticism, the Commission recommended a program by which the individual could sort out predictive statements on the basis of their significance and deal with them accordingly. Such a rational approach, however, promised more than it could deliver, for much of important decision-making is impulsive and spur-of-the-moment. Reasoning usually plays little or no part in choosing a beloved, an occupation, a residence, and even an investment. The moral of this discovery was not lost on many: we are usually victims of circumstance; rarely masters of our fate. Here, as elsewhere, we tend to deceive ourselves, thinking that we can shape the future. Such power is beyond us. Perhaps the most appropriate thing to say about the future, in the view of some cynics, is that it lies ahead.

THE LEAGUE OF UNPUBLISHED WRITERS

With the American Association of Retired Persons as a model, the League seemed to spring into existence almost overnight. Who knew there were so many scribblers toiling away in their free time? There was another similarity between the two groups. While the aged were growing in number, those who, after many years of reading stories and watching them in movies and on television, came to believe that they could tell stories as well were also becoming more numerous. Unpublished writers were everywhere, and it was time that they organized so that they could take their rightful place in society. But the new League was not well-received everywhere. Though it was not unrelated to the well-established and prosperous Authors' Guild, there was little love lost between the two organizations. The Guild looked down its corporate nose at the upstart and the League reciprocated the hostility. Such feelings were largely due to editorials by the president of the Authors' Guild in which he regularly referred to those in the League as "the unwashed," as if all its members were part of a Hindu caste system. Reciprocating, the League referred to the Guild's president in the feminine, a choice of invective that hardly reflected well on him and those he represented.

Membership fees were low and the League's ranks grew quickly in spite of the fact that joining meant announcing one's failure to achieve the traditional writer's goal. Nevertheless, there was strength in numbers. Again following the path of the AARP, which was essentially insurance-based, the League arranged for low cost group insurance for its members. Offsetting the large numbers, of course, were those unpublished writers who (mirabile dictum!) were suddenly published, automatically ending their memberships. But these represented the tiniest of numbers and their departure was hardly noticed.

Given its size, it was inevitable that the League would become a political force. It was not long before the leadership created its own detailed lobbying agenda and went on the offensive. Similarly, its size had economic consequences. No sooner did one become a member than the unsolicited mail begin to pour into his or her mail box for the League was diligent in keeping its direct mail and other advertisers up to date on membership.

Membership had its benefits. Unpublished writers, often on modest budgets, were pleased to find that they were entitled to reduced prices for such items as computers, printers, printer ink and paper. There was also a legal department that stood ready to provide advice in connection with copyright issues and the negotiation and drafting of contracts with publishing houses. As was to be expected, however, the people in this department generally had very little to do.

In time, the League's leadership attempted to sort out its membership according to their unpublishability. For cosmetic purposes, this was said to be a ranking of publishability, although few failed to see it for what it really was: a way to sideline the poorest writers completely. This led to an uproar, for it effectively stigmatized many sensitive writers who had already been identified as failures by publishers and literary agents.

Perhaps as a corrective measure, writing classes were begun, and although there were many who felt beyond such instruction, the reputation of well-known writing schools elsewhere helped bring in a fair number of students. The reading of stories was a regular part of these classes, unfortunately, for the public presentation of the work of some of the unpublished writers could be appalling. Not only might there be an almost complete absence of characterization and plot in many of these pieces, the rules of grammar often seemed to have been suspended and spelling could be awful. Nor were these students suffering from shyness; some were so taken with themselves and their work, that they would read, on and on, without interruption, until the teacher, in desperation, would be forced to shut them down, recalling, for some of the elderly in the class those vaudeville performers who had to be physically removed from the stage with a large hook.

Other steps were taken. Groups were formed following the traditional forms that creative writing took. There was, for example, one for poetry, another for nonfiction. The very large fiction group was subdivided into such units as science fiction, historical romance, etc. Other organizational distinctions followed. A Gold Club honored those who had persevered as unpublished writers for at least 15 years (later raised to 20). The president was often heard to boast about the hundreds of self-addressed-return-envelopes that brought his rejected manuscripts back home. He claimed that he used some of this great number to paper the walls of his bathroom.

Members were invited to meet regularly for the purpose of socializing and exchanging views. Although well-intended, these sessions tended to break down into bickering, each writer boasting about his own work criticizing that of others, often in the most poisonous of terms.

Just as successful writers often used literary agents to represent them in their dealings, the ranks of the unpublished writers swarmed with agents. But these were not conventional agents. Their principal activity was the reading and evaluation of the unpublished work, presumably, for the purpose of choosing that which was publishable, or advising the writers of deficiencies and suggesting how they might be remedied. All of this, of course, was done for a fee which was, at least in the agents' point of view, the main purpose. Careful examination was later to show that the considerable body of work done by these scurrilous agents yielded not a single story that made it into publication, confirming the suspicions of many writers that dealing with these agents could never lead to publication.

While considered a collection of losers by some, the League did constitute a proving ground for success in collateral fields. More than a few of its members made the transition from fiction, poetry and biography into such related professions as advertising, public relations and even the law. Putting their word skills to good use, some former League members rose quite high in those fields even if their resume's were invariably silent about their writing careers.

Eventually, however, the League fell victim to a force that was being felt in many quarters—technological change. Self-publishing, as it is now known, had only recently come on the scene. It is true, however, that a primitive antecedent had been around for a very long time. Known as Vanity Publishing, it was essentially publishing at a price, usually with few redeeming features. The bar was so low here that a manuscript could become a hard-bound book even if it consisted of nothing more than a random collection of letters of the alphabet. As Vanity Publishing evolved into Self-Publishing however, it became more respectable. Some self-published books were of first rate quality, a number were reviewed by well-known critics and a few even became best sellers.

This and other changes signaled the beginning of the end of the League of Unpublished Writers. Membership steadily declined into insignificance. It is perhaps an over-simplification to say that the League's members paid the price and became published authors with all that that signifies. More likely, a subtle, but profound change took place in the minds and sensibilities of the members; with better technology now available, including new word-processing programs, they gathered their forces, trimmed over-long sentences, sharpened characterizations, eliminated that which was trite, and, in sum, improved the quality of their work considerably. As a result, many more became published authors. Of few organizations can it be said that, like the League of Unpublished Writers, its demise was but a signpost of its members' success.

THE SCHADENFREUDE SOCIETY

This is a missionary organization, although its purpose is not a religious one. Rather, it seeks to spread the word about the benefits of a certain kind of behavior and convert as many people as possible of its advantages. The pleasure one feels about others' troubles, so effectively captured by the German word that joins the two elements, varies from person to person. That alone suggests that it can be controlled, and can be increased or diminished under the right conditions. The Schadenfreude Society is committed to the view that the road to happiness often passes through the misfortunes of others; one can lead a happier life by becoming more aware of their misfortunes and strengthening one's response to them. At the entrance to its office one is confronted with the agency's motto in giant letters: 'THEIR PROBLEMS ARE YOUR POWER.'

From the beginning, the Society came under attack. It was nothing more than selfishness, the critics contended, and nothing to be proud of. A well-ordered society requires cooperation and mutual respect; schadenfreude is disruptive, weakening the bonds that otherwise connect us. In response, the agency argued that schadenfreude had been honed by evolution over countless generations and was nothing less than an important part of the survival instinct. Authorities on the cutting edge of evolutionary theory were cited to the effect that the pleasure one feels at another's trouble was intended to make the experience more memorable for the observer, and so insure that he or she would not make the same mistake. It was, therefore, a tactic designed for survival, one of evolution's goals. Persuasive as the arguments seemed, many doubts remained.

In its plan to swell the ranks of its members, the Society set about finding those believed to have the greatest potential for conversion. In general, these were those people who thought of themselves as altruists. A convenient system for identifying those men and women consisted of sifting through the records of the major charitable organizations and listing the names and addresses of those who contributed more than the average to them. The staff was convinced that schadenfreude was the principal force behind those gifts, although they admitted that tax deductibility might be a factor.

The Society's plan of action had two parts. The first was broad-gauged and sought to educate the public as to the virtues of schadenfreude through institutional advertisements in the print media, a website, and a speakers bureau, the members of which were continuously on tour throughout the country. Its activities here followed a path that had been well-marked by such predecessors as Dale Carnegie, Ayn Rand, Eckhardt Toll and Tony Robbins.

The second part began with an invitation sent out to thousands to attend a schadenfreude event at various hotels in major cities. Included in this event were an elaborate dinner with an open bar, a program featuring known entertainers, and a talk about the advantages of schadenfreude—why everyone owes it to him- or her-self to learn more about it. The event was free, of course, as was the course of instruction that followed for those who signed up. While the course began in a classroom only a brief period was spent there. Most of the time was devoted to field trips to a variety of places where, in the judgment of the instructors, the students could best strengthen their schadenfreude responses. In general, this meant spending considerable time in various institutions, including orphanages, those caring for the needy and disabled, and hospitals. At the hospitals a gradual approach was taken, so that the class first wandered through the wards of those who were not seriously sick and might not even be bed-bound. Then, they passed on to the more serious cases, eventually arriving at the Intensive Care Unit where they spent the most time, including the time spent in the waiting rooms with the bereaved friends and loved ones of the critically ill patients. Where possible, they tried to be in attendance when last rites were administered. The theory behind this elaborate training regimen was that the schadenfreude response, while consisting, at the lowest level, of tissues, blood and neurons, could be improved in the same way that other bodily functions could—repeatedly exposing one to the appropriate stress. In their view, it was not unlike lifting weights to become stronger.

From the hospitals the trainees passed on to funeral homes and places of worship. To the credit of the Society, no distinction, advantage or discredit was made based on the religious persuasion represented by each of these institutions. Other field trips exposed the group to the worst slums in major cities and the sites of recent disasters. The buses used became a common presence and with the growing popularity of these trips the travel industry created a separate section devoted to them.

If this program seems rather straightforward, lacking in challenge, and bloodless when described in this manner, the actual events were quite different. Those enrolled as schadenfreude trainees often experienced considerable emotional distress while visiting these places of suffering, death and grieving. More than a few were reduced to tears and some were so overcome that they were forced to leave. In its defense, the Society said that the worthy end justified these difficult means. The program strengthened those who went through it and made them better men and women. In each case, they became quicker at identifying another's difficulties and their own schadenfreude responses became stronger and longer-lasting.

Like most training, this program led to a certificate of accomplishment. Those who earned certification were entitled to add "BSch" after their names. For those who pursued graduate studies in the discipline, it was possible to earn a master's degree, and then a doctorate. It was from this group that the Society selected many of its new missionaries.

THE COMMITTEE ON THE SUPPRESSION
OF PUNS

Punning had become intolerable. A random survey of some newspapers one morning yielded the following headline horrors:

"Drink Tea, Officials Say, as Britons Pour Doubt on Alcoholic Guidelines."

"Holy Mackeral! Japanese Sushi Chain Drops $117,000 For 1 Tuna."

"Causes of Crises? For Rio Governor, Life incriminates Art." (A painting is blamed for a public health emergency, plunging oil royalties and a rise in muggings)

"From Tucks to Pucks" (A plastic surgeon by day, a hockey team doctor at night)

Nor was the punning confined to headlines. In a story about compulsory union membership, a math teacher was quoted saying "The system does not add up." The crossword puzzles featured in the newspapers were not safe from the invasion. Very often the correct answer could be found only if the clue was read as a pun.

Q: Place to be in the hot seat. A: Sauna

Q: Amtrak guess, for short. A: ETA

Q: Cab suppliers. A: Winesellers.

A feature entitled "You Gotta Laugh" in the AARP Bulletin, a periodical with an enormous readership also used the Q and A format:

Q: Why do cows have hooves? A: Because they lactose.

Q: What's the difference between a hippo and a Zippo? A: One is heavy and the other is a little lighter.

Even tee shirts were pressed into service: "Oh, the hue-mana-tee," read one below an image of the multi-colored animal.

There seemed to be an epidemic of punning. More and more people began to exhibit the symptoms. First, there was a vacant look and a slack-jawed expression as the would-be punster's mind riffled through similar sounds and possible words, as if he was spinning a mental Rolodex file, and then, after the pun had been delivered, came the proud grin and the immodest question: "Did you get it?" Since most puns were sophomoric, the question was rather annoying, implying that those in the group were too dumb to understand the pun and had to be prodded.

The practice had become so widespread and its implications so serious it was inevitable that the government would act. The legislative debate was fierce. While some thought the regulation of speech was inappropriate, others proposed that habitual punsters be registered and required to undergo counseling. If they persisted in punning, they would be forced to wear an electric bracelet that would deliver a painful shock whenever they uttered a pun. As a compromise the legislature created this committee, a body that, it was hoped, would deal with the problem in a more civilized fashion.

Once organized, the Committee set out to raise the public's awareness of the extent to which paronomasia had invaded public discourse and how its widespread use had disfigured the language. At first, the Committee attempted to place advertisements in major newspapers listing and discussing notably bad puns and making the case against them. This proved difficult, however, for many of the puns criticized had appeared in the same newspapers, and the editors were uncooperative. To make sure that its message would go out to the public, the Committee fell back on its website where it began the practice of "outing" punsters much as, in earlier times, closeted homosexuals had been "outed." A professional writer was hired to develop a book of memorably awful puns.

While those basic efforts were going on, the Committee began the more significant offensive—showing how puns rarely—if ever—conveyed any original meaning, but simply repeated a point already made, and, even worse, often amounted to nothing more than bafflegab, the kind of mindless playing with the sounds of words that may be heard in nurseries, but was inappropriate for serious discourse among educated adults. Punning, it was argued further, rarely rose to the level of true wit. In fact, it could be more properly assessed as a failed attempt to be witty. Such a campaign seemed a natural topic for columnists, but here, too, difficulties were encountered. Those prestigious members of the Fourth Estate turned out to be punsters themselves, for the most part, and were reluctant to give up what they thought were some of the sharpest arrows in their quivers. Wasn't this further evidence, as if that was needed, of the punning epidemic?

In further search for an objective method by which the amount of valid information, if any, contained in each pun could be expressed, the Committee developed a scale of values, ranging from 1 to 8. At the lowest levels, the pun contained no information or very little. Such a grade might have been assigned to the tinted marine mammal we met above. At the other end there might be considerable information. An example might be the "affluenza" defense offered in court by a young man charged with murdering his parents based on the theory that, having been raised in a wealthy home, he was unable to distinguish right from wrong, and could not have appreciated the significance of his act. It was the Committee's hope that this scale would facilitate its work, allowing for concentration on the worst puns. The results however, were not clear. While some punsters saw the light and gave up punning, a larger number persuaded themselves that their puns approached the top levels where wit began and were encouraged to persevere.

The scale was followed by an even more radical project. On the Committee's website a feature appeared entitled "The Pun Hall of Shame." It did not pass notice that a regulatory body opposed to punning was actually showcasing its own pun. Some thought it ironic, others idiotic. In fact, however, it resulted from a deliberate decision to gain attention for a subject that might otherwise have escaped the notice of busy people. Such a dramatic reversal, it was hoped, demonstrated the influence of punning. If, as some members of the Committee liked to say, they were engaged in a war against puns, this had been a surprise raid into enemy territory, one that was effective, and in which no losses had been sustained.

The Committee also sought to criticize punning as bad behavior. Towards this end, staff members writing under assumed names, sent letters to etiquette columnists complaining about puns they had heard and making the argument that they were gaffes. The subject, of course, was also taken up regularly on the Committee's website.

Since continued funding for the Committee's work depended on some evidence of effectiveness, the staff felt it necessary to take polls concerning the use of puns. The first of these polls disclosed that a whopping 47.6% of those polled felt that they were capable of delivering a good pun and no less than 37.1% claimed to have delivered one within the past three days, a figure that confirmed the extent of the habit across the population. The Committee was dismayed; even they did not realize that the practice was so widespread. It was hoped that subsequent polls would show declining percentages, but in spite of the best efforts of the agency, the results were disappointing, evidence, it was said, of how strong the habit had become.

Having acquired a taste for statistics, the Committee renewed and broadened its polling activities and began adding IQ tests. The results were remarkable. Punsters generally registered IQs significantly below average. Some interpreted this finding as evidence that punning was a symptom of mental deficiency. Although the testing was criticized for its limited sampling, the results proved to have a dampening effect on punning. Those who may have been in the habit of delivering a pun now held back, perhaps unwilling to draw attention to what was sometimes seen as evidence of a mental disability.

It was years before the Committee seized upon a tactic that would be effective in curbing the enthusiasm for punning, one that was subtle and devious. Instead of attacking the practice directly, the Committee used its resources to gain public attention for instances of true wit. This was not easily accomplished since the intellectual caliber of most public discourse was low, but over time, by publicizing witty remarks, they created a frame of reference in which the poor quality of puns as wordplay could be appreciated, if only by comparison with true wit.

THE DEPARTMENT OF DRIVERLESS MOTOR VEHICLES

The DMV, the familiar Department of Motor Vehicles, this agency's predecessor, eventually closed up when the last vehicle driven by a human, in this case an octogenarian woman in Ocala, Florida, was put up on blocks. The revolution had, of course, been coming on for some time, and it was long ago that pedestrians would stand by the roadside, their mouths open in astonishment, as they saw the first driverless cars speeding past them, the passengers sometimes sitting in the back playing cards or knitting.

In the early stages of the transformation the cars were equipped with collision sensors, first with respect to backing up only, and then with respect to all motion. Similarly, there were systems for automatically maintaining an appropriate highway speed, as well as connections to global positioning satellites. A manual override was available, testimony, some said, to lingering doubt about how safe these robotic cars were. An internet connection enabled occupants to send and receive e-mail as well as research such urgent questions as the population of Australia in 1850 and dwell on pornography.

The complete change from vehicles driven by humans to those in which they were only passengers was accompanied by a change in administrative agencies. As the Motor Vehicle Department (MVD) shed staff and developed cobwebs, the new Department of Driverless Motor Vehicles (DDMV) took over.

The process was evolutionary, but it was well to remember that there was precedent. When the first automobiles first appeared, they were forced to share the road with horse-drawn carriages, horseback riders and pedestrians who felt every bit as entitled to the right of way as the new gas buggies. The friction among these competitive claimants for public space eased and eventually disappeared as cars took over simply by their numbers. A similar development is to be expected with the driverless cars: in time they will rule the roadways by virtue of their multitude although it is likely that they will more likely resemble buses than the old family sedan. The latter, which could represent the family's second largest purchase, was often treated with affection, a feeling that the new driverless car could not elicit.

The transformation had considerable economic and social consequences. Car manufacturing shrank, resulting in substantial unemployment and private car ownership was eventually replaced by publicly owned vehicles that looked like and operate like buses on flexible routes formed as needed by those with cell phones who called them up and directed them on to their destinations. Even the appearance of traffic changed as the many styles of cars once seen were eventually replaced by the single form dictated by the Department.

The Department of Driverless Motor Vehicles grew in size and importance as its administrative forebear, the Department of Motor Vehicles, shrank and eventually disappeared. In time, the new agency's symbol became one of the most familiar of images—a red steering wheel crossed by a red diagonal—as the jurisdiction of the DDMVD grew.

Because the new automobiles are more complex than their predecessors, the Department required that they should be inspected semi-annually and that special attention given to the complex new operating systems. These changes proved a boon for the auto mechanic. Traditionally, a respectable, but modest, trade characterized by grease-stained overalls and cluttered garages, it evolved over time into a more professional occupation in which its members wore white lab coats, adorned with what looked like a kind of stethoscope, were certified after a fairly rigorous training program and became entitled to add the letters CDCE after their name ("Certified Driverless Car Expert"). Their training and certification was also handled by the new Department of Driverless Motor Vehicles.

With the passing of manual operation, the design of the driverless car went through some marked changes. Storage capacity swelled and the location of seats changed. The dashboard migrated, sometimes to a panel on the side, sometimes up on the ceiling, where it often lost much of what it once provided—speed, rpms, turn-signal indicator—since there were now no humans in control who needed this data. The horn refused to die, however. To be more accurate, the absence of horns on the new driverless cars was greeted with such an uproar, that they were reinstated, but with modifications. The occupant of a driverless car could still press a button and hear a horn sound, but it was audible only within the vehicle where it continued to serve its main purpose: allowing one to vent his irritation without disturbing the serenity of the road. But these were transitory changes, features of the earliest driverless private cars before they gave way to conveyances that were more like buses.

Other adjustments that were more psychological than mechanical had to be made. For those whose driving habits included flooring the gas pedal to lead a pack of cars in accelerating away from a stop light or sign, or those who refused to keep right but drove only on the left, passing, lane, riding in a driverless car, with its own program, could be a tense experience responsible for sending more than a few to the psychiatrist's couch.

Since truck and bus drivers increasingly found themselves out of work national unemployment rose. Taxis gradually disappeared as well reducing the number of cars on crowded city streets, but adding further to the ranks of the jobless. These tendencies were more than balanced by the positive results flowing from the driverless car. Commuting to work became more efficient and, long term, the exurbs became the new suburbs.

Planners who tried to anticipate the changes produced by the disappearance of the driver were taken by complete surprise in the case of alcohol consumption. Almost overnight, the interior of the car became seen as a kind of rolling bar, perhaps a cousin of the suburban railroad bar car. Drinking on the road took off even among those who were only occasional drinkers. Freed from the need to operate the controls, those in the car felt compelled to party. And why not? They were in good hands, even if those hands were but mechanical and electronic. "DUI," or driving under the influence, seemed a curiously antique event, but, if it had disappeared, it had been replaced by an avalanche of drunkenness on the roads. In New Jersey, an experiment conducted by state troopers disclosed that 70% of the occupants of driverless cars they stopped at random over a 6 hour period failed to pass a modified breathalyzer test. This was a staggering development; It seemed as if public intoxication had exploded on the highways. The situation was so serious that the Surgeon General took to the media to issue a warning. The makers of alcoholic beverages, however, saw it as an opportunity and launched a series of advertising campaigns in which attractive men and women were shown tippling in sleek, convertible cars, racing down the highway under a starry night. The implication was that the two activities, drinking and riding in a car, seemed to go together naturally, like wine and cheese.

The response might have been expected. People like those who had made Prohibition a celebrated era in United States history quickly appeared in large numbers, as if they were cicadas suddenly and mysteriously appearing everywhere after sleeping underground for many years. But what was the offense? Driving under the influence could not be alleged since no one was driving. Nor was it a public nuisance since the drinkers were closeted in the privacy of their cars. Efforts to pass new laws covering the situation failed as a consensus developed that the right of privacy one enjoyed at home now extended to the driverless car.

The market for used vehicles changed. It was no longer possible for a salesman to boast that a car had only been driven by an elderly lady to church on Sundays, nor was there any need to avoid a car drivenby a wild teenager who did little but race his contemporaries on the road.

The field of insurance went through a sea change as well. Traditionally, insurance had been required so that those injured in vehicular accidents caused by human error could be compensated for their personal injuries or property damage. But with the passing of the driver the human error that was the predicate for such insurance also disappeared. A legislative effort to repeal the laws requiring car insurance failed, but a new method of settling claims arose modeled on the no-fault theory found both in divorce proceedings and other insurance, here administered by the Department of Driverless Motor Vehicles. The arrangement seemed particularly appropriate since the damage or injury could no longer be attributed to human error.

Vehicular litigation changed. In actions for property damage and personal injuries each party was required to show that the vehicle's operating system was in proper working order, and had been duly inspected. During the long period when roads were occupied both by driven and driver-less cars in an accident involving both it was presumed that there had been human error. This alone accelerated the change adding to the reasons why the steering wheel had to be surrendered.

THE BETTER CONVERSATION BUREAU

"The BCB," as it came to be known, as if it had always been a familiar presence, met with some resistance at first. Many felt that since they had been conversing from infancy, they were adept at it and did not need instruction. How wrong they were. The typical conversation, as the BCB demonstrated at some length, was made up of fragmentary, often disjointed, utterances, deficient in grammar and good diction and over-burdened with clichés and personal pronouns.

To overcome that initial resistance and show how poor the average conversation was, the Bureau sent out a small army of agents equipped with the latest in miniature tape recorders. These agents seemed to be everywhere, in restaurants, in buses and subways, on the streets and in offices and theaters. The unwitting subjects of this electronic eaves-dropping campaign were usually shocked when the recording was played back to them. It went far beyond the usual disappointment one experiences at hearing the sound of one's voice: your conversation was shown to be completely lacking in good form, not to mention elegance; you talked mainly about yourself, tended to interrupt, and, as a listener, you were a failure.

Bu this campaign, which went on at some length, was only preparation for the Bureau's real activity. Once the need for improvement in this area of human relations had been demonstrated, the Bureau set up a network of training centers at which the techniques of proper conversation could be taught. Here the curriculum began with an emphasis on listening. One exercise involved pairing off those in the class. One member of each pair was designated as the speaker, the other the listener. Sometimes the speaker read from some printed material; at other times he was free to talk at will perhaps telling a story. When he had finished, his partner was then called upon to recount what he had heard. There were many who could barely retrieve the gist of what had been said, and more than a few who almost completely blacked out, and were unable to say anything. The exercise, pursued over time, was effective in breaking the common habit of dwelling on the remarks one planned to make at the next opportunity at the expense of attentive listening to what his partner had been saying.

Going beyond the focus on improved listening, the attention of the class was drawn to the widespread tendency to talk about oneself without limitation. This was more than simple boasting: it was shown that the ordinary talk of most people is heavily oriented to themselves. Here, again, the students were paired off and encouraged to engage one another in ordinary conversation. This time, however, the non-speaking partner, having worked at his listening skills, now brought them to bear for the purpose of noting how many times the speaking partner used the personal pronouns—"I," "Me," "Mine." The results usually shocked both parties, but effectively paved the way for the next exercise. Each class member was then asked to talk for a period of time during which he would try to avoid the use of those pronouns. With few exceptions, this turned out to be a difficult challenge, but with time the group showed some real improvement. As an offshoot of this activity, new electronic instruments were later made available to those interested that could monitor the conversation of the bearer and, whenever he or she uttered a personal pronoun, emit a soft warning signal accompanied by a pulsing red light. Some enterprising people tried to skirt these strictures by habitually using the plural pronoun and its possessive when they were really talking about themselves, "we," and "our" being substituted for "I," "me," and "mine." To their credit, it should be said that it took some practice at this before it could be done easily, but eventually they were exposed and, among other things, the instruments were re-programmed to make the tactic impossible.

Throughout these activities the Bureau sought to emphasize that conversation was not necessarily a matter of balance. That is, it is not essential to good conversation that the same time be given to each speaker. Sometimes, one person does most of the talking, and yet both will regard the conversation as a positive experience.

Although these efforts were usually addressed to the population at large, the younger generation was also targeted with respect to speech problems peculiar to them. One example was the repetitive use of the word "like." A fair sampling of speech among the young showed clearly that the word was plugged in here and there with alarming frequency and usually only to add rhythm or fill a space and almost never for its actual meaning. Other examples of abuse were the use of the words "whatever" and "no problem." In almost every case these words had no meaning other than to signal that the person who used them was alive, awake and participating in the conversation. It was the verbal equivalent of the rapid, slight nodding that many people automatically use when listening to someone. By now the Bureau had experience in dealing with such situations Using techniques that had already proved successful, they were able to make some progress in correcting these habits.

The next step was no less formidable than the preceding ones. To recast what you typically say in the office or over dinner to friends, relatives and associates so that it is grammatical is no small thing. Of course, it seemed artificial at first, but, as is often the case, persistence paid off. Those who benefitted were fond of telling about how they met an old friend after a lengthy absence and how astonished he or she was at the changes in his or her speech, a reaction tinged with admiration.

The final matter taken up concerned transition, or the manner in which one signals that he has finished talking and his or her partner may take over. To communicate the basic idea, the old Iroquois technique was used: a "talking stick" was provided with instructions that only the person holding the stick could talk. After practicing with this technique for some time, other procedures were tried in place of the stick including a nod of the head, the blinking of one's eyes, a hand signal, or some other gesture.

For those who went through the early phases of re-education with respect to their conversation, there was an even greater challenge—making one's talk more graceful, or, as daunting.as that may sound, how to be eloquent. This was not to be confused with the effort to make one's conversation hew more closely to the rules of grammar, but focussed instead on the style with which one spoke. Just as fluency in writing varies from person to person, however, so, too, is there variety in the gracefulness with which people talk.

Overall, then, the training was varied and rigorous. To the satisfaction of the Bureau's staff, all those who completed the training evinced real improvement in conversational skills. At the head of the class were a few who showed almost virtuosic ability.

While these courses in conversation technique were going forward, they were accompanied by others on the history of conversation. Examples ranged from Socrates in the Platonic Dialogues to Charlie Rose on today's television, both, sad to say, evincing some of the worst problems to be found in conversation, but also containing such a positive example as the film, "My Dinner With Andre," depicting a one-sided, but nevertheless admirable conversation between two men.

With better conversational skills many found that their conversations grew longer and more varied, and more enjoyable. To the extent that these changes became widespread, those in the Bureau were not above claiming that they had accomplished nothing less than a wholesale change in interpersonal relations.

THE LAMED VAV BUREAU

With technological advances this ancient myth has taken on new life in the form of an administrative agency. For ages it was simply a belief that the existence of the world depended on 36 Just Men who were mostly unaware of their special identity. It was unclear whether one was born as one of the Just, acquired that character through virtuous acts, or perhaps was arbitrarily chosen by God. In any event, the procedure has now been taken over by this Bureau. More specifically, the purpose of this agency is the identification and location of these individuals, their organization and assistance in carrying out their extraordinary mission.

An early dispute concerned the very number of the Just. Since some considered their number as a function of population, it was argued that their number should increase in proportion to the rise in the world's population. Those who subscribed to this idea had difficulty in estimating the population that existed when the Lamed Vav concept originated. Eventually, they settled on such a small figure that simple extrapolation would have produced no less than 324 hidden saints, a substantial group in itself. Perhaps inspired by this argument, some women's liberation groups protested the male-only character of the Lamed Vav. The conciliatory offer of a token woman in the group was treated with scorn; they would settle for nothing less than complete parity with the male gender.

Once such matters came under serious consideration, the way was opened for other issues. Since the entire planet's future was at stake, it seemed wrong that the Just should be limited to Jews.

All religious groups, it was said, should be represented, and then, the door having opened, should not there be representation from other races, other ethnicities, other nationalities, other age groups, and even from those with divergent sexual identities such as those who were homosexual or transgender?

With the resolution of these conceptual issues, the Bureau turned to the identification of the saints in the belief that their work could be enhanced if they were known and organized. In coming to this conclusion the staff no doubt compared ancient times with modern conditions where, among other things, the Internet can call up the most complicated and recondite information in seconds. The staff also adopted the unique procedures followed in awarding Macarthur Grants carefully keeping them secret so that it is virtually impossible to campaign for selection.

That secrecy disappeared when the Hidden Saints were finally identified, the event producing headlines and the Just instantly became celebrities. Their photos and biographies were published widely and they found themselves besieged by reporters, those who wanted to interview them, those who offered to manage their affairs and many who just wanted to be in their presence. The Bureau did what it could to protect them.

Another difficulty involved the relationship between the Lamed Vav and the government. If the world's existence depended on them, it could be argued that they constituted a kind of super-government, or perhaps an ultimate court of appeal. Here, too, the Bureau was active as a moderating force, going to great lengths to show how the the two organizations could operate harmoniously. Finally, the agency intervened on behalf of the saints when it was felt that their will had not been served.

Traditionally, the Lamed Vav were not organized. That is, each member operated alone, unaware of the others, in accordance with his individual sense of his destiny, if he was aware of it. Here the Bureau sought to make a revolutionary change, assembling the Just periodically and, following parliamentary procedures, tried to form a consensus. Since each of the Just had proceeded alone for so long, and the habit had become entrenched, this was not easily accomplished. Although these meetings were secret, there was some leakage, and the diversity of opinion could be startling. As one example, a minority argued strenuously that all of the resources of the Lamed Vav should be directed at ensuring that the Atlanta Falcons win the National Football League super bowl one year. Another time, their efforts sought to ensure that the number 373737 be picked in the New York State Lottery. It was rumored that one of the Just had that ticket. Over the years, however, these anomalies disappeared and a consensus would form more readily.

The Bureau's purpose in organizing the group was salutary: if the Lamed Vav's efforts could be orchestrated, it was said, their effectiveness could be magnified. Instead of manipulating the Super Bowl, for example, their concentrated efforts might be used to stop global warming or deflect a large meteorite that was on a collision course with earth. Even then, however, the Bureau could not escape criticism that it exhibited a holier-than-thou attitude.

In general, however, the Bureau was regarded with considerable respect. Its offices were daily visited by delegations from around the world composed of the nations' highest ranking and wealthiest citizens. These events, marked by kow-towing and extreme respect reminded some of the way in which minor vassals once abased themselves before feudal emperors or supplicants approached the Pope.

Not all of those interested in the Bureau were welcomed. Among those who were persona non grata were those who believed that there was a conspiracy behind most events, a belief that they extended to the agency. For them this arrangement harbored a secret combination run by disreputable people for their profit. The Bureau did what it could to distance itself from this view, insisting that its program was serious and beneficial while the conspiracies amounted to little more than rumor mongering.

A considerable part of the agency's time was devoted to locating successors to the Lamed Vav when one passed on. The original myth was silent on this matter, the assumption being that members were replaced in the same mysterious way that they had been chosen. In our electronic age, however, it is possible to review the credentials of all humanity, now estimated to be well above 8 billions. Of course, the process by which as few as 36 can be found in such a vast number is daunting, suggesting, if a metaphor is needed, the probability that someone with a pin can strike a beetle on a football field.

An early effort of the Bureau to follow bloodlines in replacing the Just proved a failure. One did not inherit Lamed Vav status. In the next attempt, the search was restricted to those of the Jewish faith, but the Bureau quickly realized that the concept did not admit of religious, national, ethnic or any other distinction. That is, anyone could be a member of the Lamed Vav, including the disabled elderly black man who cleans the men's room in Pennsylvania Station and makes sure that there are enough rolls of toilet paper. It was here that the Internet proved useful. As the world's population increasingly became connected through this device, it became possible to assess the qualities of each and every user. At first, this sifting involved the more or less obvious matters—gender, age, ethnicity and nationality. Then it became more finely tuned, identifying, for example, those who earned more than a certain amount of money. As the fine-tuning proceeded, it became possible to identify those who liked to play Scrabble, had a mole on his back, or did a good deed last week. Eventually, it became possible to identify those who had that magical aura that identified them as one of the Lamed Vav. There was widespread astonishment. Those who were so identified included, as well as the black bathroom attendant, an elderly Puerto Rican woman in a nursing home, a teenage boy, member of a criminal gang in Harlem, and an overweight luggage salesman in Indianapolis, Indiana.

With all these developments, the success of the Bureau and the vitality of the Lamed Vav caught the attention of the business community. Members of the group were besieged by promoters who promised big fees if they would lend themselves to the selling of everything from soap to insurance, used cars and dating services. To their credit, however, the Just refused these offers. They did prove more receptive, however, to those appeals for help from such groups as those engaged in the fight against world hunger, and the provision of medical services to the needy. In this the Bureau provided useful services as an intermediary.

The role of the Lamed Vav and the Board in the future is not entirely clear. It could be argued that as the world continues to shrink and boundaries fall, the Just are destined to play an increasingly important role in world affairs. In that case, this Bureau will certainly grow in influence.

THE SOLITARY SECURITY ADMINISTRATION

For many years, the percentage of single households had been climbing. Contributing to this trend was the graying of the population, a decline in the number of marriages, and rising income levels that eased the need for more than one wage-earner. That more and more people lived alone spoke of a major change in society; among other things, it meant that more people experienced great loneliness. In personal advice columns and elsewhere complaints were heard of men and women who went for days without talking to another person, sometimes going so far as to shop for an unneeded item only to exchange a few words with the salesperson. In earlier times when farming was a large part of the economy and many lived close to the earth and distant from his neighbors, solitude was accepted. Now, ironically, when most of us live close to one another in dense urban areas, it had become a problem.

It was against this background that the Solitary Security Administration was created. Its charter recited, in rather melodramatic language, how loneliness was a mighty foe, not to be underestimated, one capable, no less, of unravelling the fabric of society, but that it would be vanquished at all costs. The coming battle was compared to those in which such major diseases as infantile paralysis, typhoid fever and malaria were conquered. Overlooked in such brave talk was the ambiguity of the agency's title; as some critics pointed out, one might be solitary without being lonely. In the wake of that criticism, a surprising number of people felt it necessary to give testimony to the fullness of their solitary lives.

There were musicians and writers, knitters and modelers, painters and puzzle enthusiasts, all anxious to describe how busy they were while alone.

Among its first activities the Administration sent hundreds of trained agents into the field to meet many of the lonely, examine their situation and measure the severity of their condition. In this, the Administration was acting much like the Visiting Nurse Service that sends trained nurses to those home-bound individuals in need of medical attention or those home care agencies that provide non-medical assistance for the same groups, or even, perhaps, like Meals on Wheels. Generally well-received, these agents engaged the subject in conversation at some length and made observations of his or her dress and behavior, the condition of the home, its tidiness, how well things were organized, etc. No conclusions were drawn at that meeting, but back at the office the agent applied certain formulas to produce a determination that came to be known as The Loneliness Quotient (LQ) which was the basis for all later action. To take that measure each agent used a battery of 20 questions such as "Do you feel starved for company?" and "Is it difficult for you to make friends?" A triage policy was in effect pursuant to which those with the greatest LQs were dealt with first.

Those chosen became eligible for a monthly allowance that varied in relation to the severity of the condition. At first, recipients were free to dispose of the allowance in any way they liked. Some spent it on clothes or household goods, others on entertainment or travel, but most treated it as an endorsement of their lonely life style. In time, the Administration became more vigilant, taking steps to insure that the allowance was used exclusively to combat loneliness and make more secure the lives of those who had become disabled by loneliness. Every 6 months the allowance was reviewed, at which time it could be revised up or down or even terminated. According to the Internal Revenue Service, the allowance was not taxable income, a circumstance that added considerably to its appeal.

One would think that there would be a certain amount of manipulation by those being interviewed as they sought to qualify for these desirable payments, but the agents were sophisticated and adept at dealing with such ploys. Nevertheless, lie detectors were sometimes used by special agents who also made surprise visits to check the validity of earlier determinations. When wild parties were disclosed as a result of several of such visits the agency was able to secure press coverage that acted as a caution to other would-be malefactors.

The program was criticized by conservatives who called it just another kind of hand out and an unjustified incursion into private life. Its defenders pointed out that it was essentially like Workers Compensation or the Social Security System's disability provisions, but that it involved the individual's emotional life which could be equally disabling.

Those denied a Loneliness Allowance could appeal the determination to an appellate body. Around that agency a small body of lawyers developed who specialized in such matters. They liked to be called the "Lonesome Bar," perhaps because that title evoked images of the wild west and cowboys packing six guns.

Upon certification by the Administration, there were other consequences besides the financial. Individuals so registered could expect regular telephone calls and e-mails inquiring about their circumstances, as well as follow-up visits every four months.

Possibly due to the publicity concerning the Administration, a number of people saw a competitive potential in solitude. That is, the question was: who can remain solitary for the longest period of time? An organization was created to oversee the events and promulgated appropriate rules. Solitude had to be defined. Among other things, was one's solitude affected by a telephone call or a door-to-door salesman? Did such events end one's solitude, or only interrupt it? How about e-mail? Once these matters were settled, a surprising number of people joined the contest. Since it was self-policing, there was always some doubt about the veracity of the claims, especially because, in time, the periods during which some people claimed to be solitary stretched so long as to become implausible. Some contestants tried to bolster their claims with the testimony of a spouse or significant other with whom he or she lived. That, in turn, created a dispute as to whether a member of such a household could be said to be solitary. Some of those in this group noted, ironically, that living under the same roof with his or her mate was essentially living alone.

The lonely life led to strategic thinking in other ways. A common problem for the person navigating the shoals of single living arose when he or she dined in a restaurant. The greeting of the host or hostess—"Just one?"—was so full of disapproval that it often cast a pall over the occasion and ensured that there would not be a return. To deal with this problem a ploy was in use said to be developed by an elderly retired lawyer with a considerable reputation as a curmudgeon. When dining out he carried an inflatable doll that he blew up before entering, turning some formless rubber into the semblance of a pretty young girl with a dazzling smile. Then, arm in arm with her, he presented himself to the host. "Two, please," he said firmly. While the host or hostess was usually dumbstruck at first, he or she would usually gather himself or herself, and with a mechanical smile, say "This way, please." Those who used this strategy were full of praise for it, claiming that their rubberized companions were perfect: they looked beautiful, never had a hair out of place, never argued with you, ate very little, did not use the bathroom, were the cheapest of dates, and, if they ever did something to annoy you, could be quickly deflated and put away.

The restaurant scene was a major target for the Administration. A study disclosed that most restaurants are designed and furnished for couples and that communal eating places are rare. Steps were taken to creae more such places, sometimes with financial aid, and the agency did what it could to secure good reviews for them.

As the agency grew into a familiar feature on the regulatory landscape, its formal name faded and it became known as "The Loneliness Administration, a name that seemed a better fit given that "solitary" and "solitude" refer to a physical condition and do not reach the psychological and emotional consequences of that isolation. And yet there were those to whom the original word seemed more appropriate since, in their view, human life, no matter what turns it takes, is essentially a solitary experience.

THE DEPARTMENT OF DEATH

N ot that long ago, death was an unmentionable subject, like sex had been. "What's the point?" people would say; or, "You're dead—period." Then came the sexual revolution and even the most intimate matters were discussed. As if it was following that pattern, death, too, emerged into ordinary conversation. Now, death was not merely life's conclusion, it was complex and afforded many possibilities for imagination, analysis, meditation, conversation and more.

One of the first steps taken during this gradual change was the death café, a monthly social gathering that quickly spread around the world. The topics under discussion at these meetings were not limited to death, of course, and many participants only occasionally talked about the titular subject. These cafes did, however, represent a breakthrough, however, a setting in which one might find it possible to talk about what had been a forbidden subject.

Once the end of life had taken a larger place in the public consciousness, it was inevitable that a public agency would eventually be created to deal with some of its more significant issues. That was a considerable change in itself, since, traditionally, the only way in which an agency dealt with the subject of death was in certifying its occurrence and the precipitating causes. The agency charged with this duty was the awkwardly named Department of Health.

The jurisdiction of the new department extended beyond the simple certification of life's terminal event. Among its activities the agency provided training, assistance in suicide and obituary writing and even organized gatherings at which attendees tried to communicate with the dead. The training sessions, which were provided free of charge, aimed at familiarizing older people who would not have had the high school course on the subject, with the organic changes that occur as death approaches, and, beyond that event, the decomposition and disfiguring of the body as it is transformed, finally, into a skeleton, all in rather grisly detail. Vital as was the information provided, and even though it was free of charge, these sessions were, at first, rarely attended by more than a handful of people who usually sat without expression, as if they were undergoing some uncomfortable examination. This was to change, in time, as the Department became more influential.

With the passing of the older generation, the Department concentrated its training activities on high school students in their senior year. The assumption was that these young people were in their prime and had sufficient vitality to withstand the awful details of their decline and death. Fears that the students would be taken to a morgue to examine corpses proved unfounded. In fact, the course was handled sensitively; there were no reports of tears or fainting, and it appeared that the level of attention and interest among the students was unusually high.

The Department also provided assistance in the writing of one's obituary. Here, new ground was broken since, by tradition, the obituary had been written by a third person, usually a specialist, after the subject had died. That the individual himself could have a hand in the writing of his obituary struck some as revolutionary; others thought it a contradiction in terms. But the change was well received by those who took part, evidence, some said, that the old procedure was unsatisfactory. It seems more likely, however, that the interest in auto-obituary writing, as it came to be known, was due to the fact that it was closely related to the memoir-writing that had been in vogue for decades. For those who felt that they were not up to the task, the department provided trained representatives who helped in the writing.

The nature of the obituary changed as well. Since the subject was still alive, some part of the piece was speculative, and, very often, nothing more than wishful thinking. Similar distortions could be made out in the recounting of one's past, as many sought to cover themselves with glory where that could not be justified, or failed to acknowledge serious mistakes made or great opportunities lost. While most of these pieces hewed to a simple chronology, some of the writers, exhibiting a more poetic sensibility, made space in their accounts for memorable thoughts and emotions, and dramatic scenes and actions.

Since the subjects of these obituaries continued in existence, they were no longer shielded by that special regard accorded to the dead. Errors and exaggerations in the author's account were easy targets and some often found that they had become fair game for ridicule. Since the obituary had become a work in progress, so to speak, more than a few authors responded positively to well-founded criticism and rewrote their pieces accordingly.

The new obituary writing was open to all, regardless of age or medical condition, and there were some teenagers and even younger children who tried their hands at it, but, for the most part, the writers were those who knew it was the right time due to an event that reminded them dramatically of life's uncertainty, perhaps a serious illness, a hospital stay, the death of a relative or friend or a close call with a truck while crossing the street.

Other functions were the messenger registry, group training for the event, and suicide assistance. The registry was for those convinced that, once deceased, they would be able to communicate with those who had preceded them into the afterlife. This group, which met regularly, was surprisingly large, and not a little varied. In it were those who believed they would be able to converse with the dead just as if they met them on the street or sat across from them at breakfast. Some were certain that any such message had to be printed, or at least written on paper if it was to be communicated. Still others, perhaps motivated by paper's impermanence, were convinced that such messages had to be chiseled in stone, preferably marble. And yet others felt that the proper medium was metal. Even here there was partisanship, for those who voted for metal could not agree on the right kind of metal. Some felt that high quality steel was a must; others were convinced copper was needed; still others argued that bronze was required because of traditional reasons. No matter the medium of the message, there was agreement among all that it had to be delivered manually, a physical transfer from one to another. In accordance with these beliefs, arrangements were made that these physical texts accompany the deceased's body whether interred or cremated. As to these and all other matters concerning messages in the afterlife the department provided thoughtful assistance.

The group training given was much like the yoga and tai chi group activities that have become common in larger cities. Here the participants usually reclined, closed their eyes, and, following the instructions of a leader, tried to imagine dying and then tried to penetrate the veil that is said to descend with that event. There was no lack of testimony from those who claimed to have had extraordinary experiences in these sessions.

In addition to these training activities, the agency arranged for the construction of an imposing sign In New York City's Times Square that kept a running total of the world's annual deaths starting on January 1st. This was modeled, no doubt, on the similar sign that displayed the world's population. In time, it became customary for one of the major television stations to end its daily broadcasting with a view of that sign.

The department's role in suicide eventually became considerable. The agency was careful not to violate the laws of any jurisdiction in which the event was to take place and the agency was also diligent in keeping up with any change in medical procedure that might be relevant. Within these restrictions the would-be suicide could choose from a long list of options as to method, site, décor, publicity, music, attendance, and so forth. Certain suicides, because of their grandeur, were sometimes covered by the news media, especially if they involved celebrities.

Because cremation had increasingly replaced burial in the ground or interment elsewhere, the nature of funerals gradually changed over time. In the absence of the deceased's body or a gravestone, those bereaved eventually came to regard the date of death in the same way that birthdays or marriage anniversaries are celebrated. This was a major change with implications for funeral homes, florists, the gift card industry, and others. The observation of the anniversary of one's death became common behavior. In its monthly bulletin the Department of Death provided advice on subtle questions of etiquette with respect to the observation of these dates.

The agency was not without its critics who complained that it had a morbid influence on affairs; to affirm life, they argued, we must ignore death; in effect they wanted to make the subject unmentionable again. But such progress is irreversible, and death would forever more remain out in the open.

THE EXTINCTION INSTITUTE

It is often said of this entity that it looks both to the past and to the future: in one capacity, it records those species that have already died off; in the other, it anticipates the coming extinction of those that are still alive. The appearance of such a Janus-faced agency to deal with extinction issues, was a long time coming, especially because, as some critics pointed out, we—our species—have been responsible for many, if not most, of the extinctions that have occurred in modern times, and, until recently, we have been unwilling to acknowledge our guilt. That changed with the growth of ecological awareness. This is, after all, the Anthropocene, that time in the geological life of our planet, when humanity has become, perhaps, the principal shaping force in the biosphere, a force that has driven many other species into extinction. While those species have disappeared, ours has exploded; the world's human population, now estimated to be 7.4 billion, is expected to rise to 11.2 billion by 2100. With such vast numbers, many other species that share our common habitat, find themselves in impossibly crowded conditions, threatened with a similar fate.

In general, the Institute seeks to increase awareness of extinction as the natural end of evolution; more specifically, it seeks to account for those extinctions that have been produced by humanity. Without that limitation, the job of dealing with such events going back to primordial times would have been impossible, so multitudinous were those species that have passed across the face of the earth and disappeared. Even with that limitation, however, the agency's files are enormous. To a certain extent, the Institute tries to memorialize those lost creatures. Through its website, installations in natural history museums and a series of lectures the images and habits of some of those extinct animals, birds, insects and fish are kept alive in the public mind.

But it is with impending and future extinctions that the Institute is more fully engaged, a task that is daunting for a number of reasons. Extinction does not occur instantly and dramatically, but takes place gradually, its onset usually not observed until that critical point when the remaining population is too small for the species to continue, and it then spirals down into oblivion. In its effort to anticipate the earliest beginnings of this process, the Institute developed formulas for breeding populations that factored in a long list of conditions including natural predators, climate change, and, of course, as noted, the overwhelming presence of humanity.

From these preliminary comments it should be clear that this agency's principal duties are the monitoring of those forces that combine to extinguish a species, calling the public's attention to that phenomenon and then trying to preserve the species. These are difficult tasks, in part because of the common tendency to think of extinction as something that occurred in the age of the dinosaurs and has no application here and now, whereas the forces that lead to extinction are in operation all around us. To accomplish its work the Institute relies on the public at large and the interest many individuals have in participating in a scientific project. When a species is declared to be endangered, any and all sightings are listed together with the names of those calling them in. When, later, the species is declared to be critically endangered, the listings take on an even more urgent tone. Although the celebrity attached to this attribution is modest, it proved to be a powerful inducement, and elicited a surprising number of callers. In time, the arrangement took on the character of a perverse contest, the participants vying to be the person who made the last sighting and gaining lasting renown. On its website the agency employs a kind of countdown, the endangered species being listed together with the current number of each. When a species finally passes into extinction, the event is newsworthy and is dramatized with funereal music and a blackened screen.

But the Institute also does what it can to bring back endangered species from the brink of oblivion. In this regard, it is active in protecting the members of such a species from its natural predators, going so far as to build and maintain enclosures for them, although they were warned that such steps could very well threaten natural balances. When the threat is not from predators, but from diseases, the agency provides medical care. Sensible of the fact that a species population has a critically minimum size, it sometimes takes steps to facilitate breeding, and even goes so far as to relocate as many members as possible, moving them away from their native habitat and to a friendlier environment.

Even more extreme is the Institute's effort to resurrect extinct species. Using tissue samples from dead creatures and applying newly-discovered knowledge about genetics, the agency pushes ahead to create life where it had seemed to pass from the scene. Staff members assigned to this work often liked to address each other as "Dr. Frankenstein."

But even a casual review of the Institute's activities discloses that it has a doubtful relationship with respect to evolution, in some instances seeming to operate in a contradictory fashion. The preservation and revitalization of an endangered species may well interfere with the evolutionary process. If extinction is the ultimatel end of evolutionary change—the common destination of all creatures--what happens when it is suspended, or reversed? The consequences of such meddling are still obscure. Into what new pathways will the forces of evolution be directed?

The Institute's critics, who are numerous and vociferous, aregue that the agency is playing God, a very dangerous game indeed. Here they make common cause with those who believe that each species has a biological limit and that our species long ago exceeded that assigned to it. It has become increasingly clear that the world's human population has been responsible for many problems, economic in terms of life support, aesthetic in terms of the terrestrial landscape, and theological in terms of God's divine plan.